TENNIS TACTICS

Books by Dr. Robert Ford Greene

TENNIS DRILLS

TENNIS TACTICS

TENNIS TACTICS

Match Play Strategies
That Get Immediate Winning Results

Dr. ROBERT FORD GREENE

G. P. PUTNAM'S SONS

NEW YORK

Copyright © 1978 by Dr. Robert Ford Greene

All rights reserved. This book, or parts thereof, may not be reproduced
in any form without permission from the publisher. Printed simultaneously
in Canada by Longman Canada Limited, Toronto.

SBN: 399-12120-X

Library of Congress Cataloging in Publication Data

Greene, Robert Ford.
  Tennis tactics.

  Includes index.
  I. Tennis. 2. Tennis—Psychological aspects.
I. Title.
GV995.G697   1978   796.34'22   77-26216

PRINTED IN THE UNITED STATES OF AMERICA

ACKNOWLEDGMENTS

I wish to thank the following people for their able assistance in the publication of this book:

Edward T. "Ned" Chase, senior editor at G. P. Putnam's Sons, for skillfully guiding the manuscript to fruition, with the expertness that only an accomplished tennis player is privileged.

Robert Barker, Steve Gottlieb, Ronald and Jane Rebhuhn, and Dr. Edward Schwartz, for reading the manuscript and offering constructive criticism.

Ina and Robert Caro, Rosalie Dixon, Dr. Patricia and Prof. E. Allan Farnsworth, Dr. David Ju, Quinto Vallei, Jr., and my good brother, John J. Greene, Jr., of Kenosha, Wisconsin, for encouragement along the way.

Adair Miller, for permission to be photographed at the Apple Hill Farm Condominium, in Chappaqua, New York.

Albert Guida, for his photography; Jack Luboff, for photographic artwork; and Manny Warman, who contributed two photographs.

Spalding, Inc., for generously supplying me with tennis rackets throughout the years, and Fred Perry Sportswear of New Jersey, for furnishing clothing.

My buddy and loving wife, Joan, for her enormous effort in so many ways, including the drawing of all of the diagrams that appear in this book.

I wish to dedicate this book to two very special people: Dr. Jules Stein and Mrs. Doris Stein, of Beverly Hills, California, who have touched my life so deeply, and who, by sharing a sense of concern and commitment toward their fellow man, make this a better world in which to live.

DR. ROBERT FORD GREENE
Riverdale, New York
March, 1978

PREFACE

This book is designed to help you become a smart tennis player, enabling you to win when you should, and even when you shouldn't. Regardless of whether you are a raw beginner or a touring professional, a man, woman, girl, boy, or a senior, the book will help you advance to your highest limit considering your stroking and physical capabilities. Many tactical secrets are included that have never before been seen in print.

Unlike the mastery of shots and the utilization of drills,* which require long hours of practice, the acquisition of tactics can give *immediate* results. By using the strategies explained in this book you should always defeat opponents who have inferior games; they will find it almost impossible to beat you. The strategies will also help you to pull off an upset or "steal" a match from an opponent. It is possible for an intelligent player occasionally to beat someone with superior strokes and speed afoot.

The book is intended to help produce players who are winners. In using the term "winners" I am not necessarily referring to the players who end up winning tournaments. I am talking about the man, woman, or child who extracts the maximum number of games, or victories, within the limitations of his or her racket-handling ability and physical attributes. Like a remarkable military leader such as Stonewall Jackson, who, though outgunned and outnumbered, turned imminent defeats into brilliant victories, the smart player gets unusual "mileage" out of his resources.

*My recent book, *Tennis Drills*, teaches stroke development through exercises and drills.

In tournament play I, for one, have been able to achieve success with minimal stroking equipment. Not having the "big guns," and competing at times against some of the best players in the world, I have been forced to outthink my opponents in order to remain competitive with them.

This book offers tactics in a flexible manner, so that your individual strengths and weaknesses are considered when a particular strategy is introduced. Tactics are not presented in static fashion, as they are in many other volumes; there are no directives such as "*Always* come to the net after your opponent hits a short ball inside your service line." This theory, for instance, would not be advisable if your opponent had great passing shots, or, conversely, if you had a very weak net game.

In addition to teaching tactics, this book offers many tips that should help make your tennis playing fun and rewarding. Through the use of numerous photographs and illustrations, care was taken to make the material easily understandable. Included in the book are a chapter "Guidelines for Intelligent Tennis Play," a glossary, and a tennis-court diagram.

Needless to say, the "you" in this book refers both to males and to females, except where otherwise specified. (The use of the "editorial masculine"—for example, reference to the opponent as "he"—throughout is done for the sake of simplicity.) Nowadays, not only do as many women as men play tennis; they play essentially the same types of games and, by and large, use the same tactics. Every one of us—man or woman, boy or girl, young or old—can improve tactically so as to play more effectively and win more often.

CONTENTS

INTRODUCTION

WHAT ARE TACTICS?

"Tactics," or "strategy," is a plan of action used to attain maximum results against an opponent. Good tactics help us utilize our talents in the most effective manner possible. When a player with fine tennis strokes, physical condition, and mobility loses to someone with inferior equipment, the probability is that his tactics were poor.

HOW TO USE THIS BOOK

For purposes of experiment, use your tactics first in practice matches, rather than in tournament or team competition. Concentrate on only one tactic at a time. For example, do not work on your drop shot during the same game in which you are concerned with developing anticipation of the opponent's shots. Review this book periodically and employ the strategies on three or four separate occasions, so they will automatically become part of your tennis game.

Bear in mind that the player who has the most extensive assortment of effective shots, as well as the great-est speed afoot, has the greatest number of tactical options at his disposal. Versatile, advanced players can use four or five completely different games against an opponent. Included among these are serving and volleying, playing in the backcourt and hitting groundstroke loops, and bringing an opponent to the net and passing him.

HOW TO IMPROVE

Finally, a word about self-improvement in tennis. First, develop sound strokes; then go out and, with great concentration, hit thousands upon thousands of balls toward specific targets, constantly increasing the pace on the ball. A substantial share of your hitting should be done in match play; that is, against tough players in the head-to-head competition that teaches one how to win. The smart player will reach higher plateaus and rise faster than one who neglects the cerebral aspect of the game. The use of the tactics listed in this book will help guarantee that your tennis star will rise as fast and as far as it should.

TENNIS TACTICS

Chapter **1**

MOLDING YOUR TENNIS GAME

Before dealing in depth with specific tennis tactics, it is important to discuss relative factors that determine the level of one's tennis game.

AGE

A child can develop ball skills as early as two years of age and is usually receptive to learning the game of tennis by the time he or she is eight or nine years old. And there are many men and women who play an active and competitive game through their seventies.

The person of forty who is learning the game of tennis should not use the same practice approach as the youngster of nine. (Although an older player can become very skillful, hardly anyone has become a Wimbledon or world's champion after starting to play the game intensively at an age older than fourteen or fifteen.) The older person is better off avoiding the big, powerful overspin groundstrokes, since they require too much time to master and energy to produce. If an older learner is planning to spend a considerable amount of time playing doubles, he should practice the volley regularly.

All of us must ask ourselves whether we want to spend the extra time to develop the very sound strokes that will pay off in future years, or to learn strokes that will help us win immediately. The more advanced in age we are, the shorter the payoff period for our strokes. The mature learner should be concerned with consistency and satisfaction, and should place less emphasis on the involved intricacies of form. Nevertheless, whether young or old, a player learning the game should attempt to develop proper grips and strokes.

ASPIRATIONS

When a player has high aspirations, he should accept the fact that he must work very hard in develop-

ing his tennis game. The aspiring player should obtain as much help from teaching professionals as possible. He should also read many instructional books and articles and observe good players. For the first five to seven years of his development he must be careful not to compromise by using poor stroking form for the sake of being more effective in a match. Improper form does not handicap the beginner's ability to win as much as it sets limits on his path to progress. A player with high aspirations must plan on practicing serious tennis no less than two or three hours a day, five days a week, the year round.

TIME AVAILABLE FOR PLAY

If your job or schedule is such that you can play only once or twice each week, try to keep your strokes short, and swing the racket slowly or at medium speed. Hitting a ball hard requires precise timing, and there is no way to develop and preserve that timing except to stroke hundreds of balls each week. The Saturday and Sunday player should develop just a small number of high-percentage shots (e.g., crosscourt groundstrokes that are aimed at a safe distance above the net and well inside the boundary lines) rather than frustrate himself with a wide variety of screaming slices and drives. The player who has only a minimum amount of time available should not expect outstanding results, and should accept the fact he will mishit the ball more frequently than will the chap who plays regularly.

TYPE OF JOB

Certain occupations and professions are ideal for the serious-minded tennis player. The teacher who can be ready to play at 4 P.M. daily, and who has summers and holidays free, is in an ideal position to improve his tennis game rapidly. To play the game as well as he can, a player must lead a life that is somewhat free of pressure. The player whose job is demanding is usually wisest to restrict his play to that with friends and to avoid tournaments *(Fig. 1.1)*. Tournament tennis demands a great deal of time and energy. In some ways it resembles a demanding and jealous suitor, who, when not receiving complete attention, reacts unfavorably.

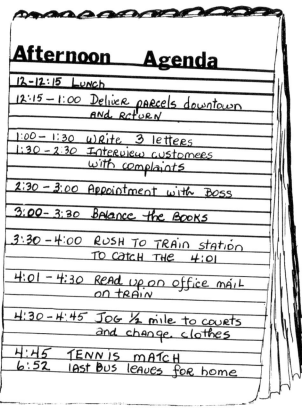

Fig. 1.1 This agenda guarantees a poor tennis performance.

FINANCIAL SITUATION

Although the game of tennis has to some extent moved from the country club to the public parks, it still favors the wealthy player over the poor. The well-to-do person can hire a professional, not only for lessons but for competition. He can afford to join country clubs, where tennis courts are more readily available, and he can purchase the finest equipment: for example, quality and resilient gut stringing instead of nylon. To the player in the northern part of the United States, to those who live in areas where there is a cold winter,

money is advantageous in purchasing indoor time, which can cost about ten to forty dollars an hour. Knowledgeable tennis players say that no player ever became extremely good without solid financial backing from a family or a tennis federation.

The player who has a limited amount of money available should not despair, however. He can play outside, in his sweatsuit, on hard courts during cold weather; utilize a backboard to develop certain shots; use money-saving and durable nylon strings in his racket; and should be able to scrape up the money to take a number of professional tennis lessons early in his career. For the average individual, the critical element in his development as a tennis player is not his income but the amount of leisure time he has available. Unfortunately, they often go hand in hand.

PHYSICAL CAPABILITY

If you are tall, you have a big advantage when playing the forecourt game and when playing doubles. You have extra reach, both on volleys and overheads. Height is also an asset in serving. Although a short player does not have the leverage on groundstrokes that a tall one does, he can usually generate plenty of power. A short person has a lower center of gravity, and thus usually has better balance, and his eyes are closer to the level of the ball. He also has better hand-eye coordination. With these three advantages, the shorter player has greater backcourt and steadiness potential.

If you are blessed with speed afoot, you can play either a hard-hitting game or a retrieving one. To be effective, the slow-footed player must use power, because when he hits the ball hard, he does not have to run as quickly. He has more time to get to his opponent's shots, since the opponent cannot return a hard ball as close to the lines with power and accuracy. Don Budge is a classic example of one who developed greatness without having unusual running speed. In his prime, Pancho Gonzales did not have the bombs off the ground that Budge had, but was blessed with such great court-covering ability that he could afford to hit a softer ball on certain shots.

A player with good size and strength should develop powerful strokes. The generation of power without strain is indeed an asset.

An important factor to consider in the molding of one's tennis game is stamina—overall physical conditioning. If you are not in particularly good shape and do not relish becoming involved in a nasty physical struggle, you should develop a game in which points do not last indefinitely. The less-fit person should seek to master the type of game in which he takes the ball earlier off the bounce, hits closer to the lines, and hits harder. A careful type of retrieving player must be in exceptional physical condition, since he often must do twice as much running as his opponent.

And, if a player has slow reflexes (owing to minimal ball experience) and/or poor eyesight, it is advisable for him to stay in the back of the court rather than near the net. By doing this, he usually has a slower ball to cope with, and one that is easier to focus on. (Many fine players have improved their vision by wearing eyeglasses or contact lenses.) Although raw reflexes cannot be improved upon, a player learns to react faster with increased muscle development.

MENTAL MAKEUP

It is fortunate when a person likes to play the kind of tennis game for which he is suited, mentally as well as physically. Occasionally one sees a player whose style of game does not utilize his natural assets. There are those who have the temperament to stroke a ball slowly and carefully, and those who like to hit hard.

People often choose the hard-hitting game compulsively. There are some players who bring aggression to the courts and expect to rid themselves of it by clobbering the devil out of the ball. In this case, they have a difficult time playing effectively, and thus their off-court problems can be further compounded.* However, there are players, including my wife, who prefer to hit hard and lose rather than push the ball slowly and win. To each his own!

If you prefer not to become overly concerned with winning and losing, you can structure your tennis so that it will not be threatening or highly competitive. You can avoid those players who bring on these feelings. Drilling is an excellent method of perfecting your game in a noncompetitive manner.

Those players who are blessed with an unusual amount of patience will find it an asset on a tennis court. They can bide their time while waiting for an

*On- and off-court anger was one of the topics dealt with in an experimental course entitled "Tennis Values and Human Values," which I initiated at CCNY for members of the varsity-tennis team.

opening; the impatient player cannot. Players who lack self-control find playing a retrieving type of game extremely unnerving.

HOME-COURT SURFACE

The type of court surface you will likely play on most of your life should be an important consideration when planning your game. There are some readers on the west coast of the United States who will probably never play on any surface other than a hard court, and they should mold their games accordingly. On hard courts the serve, volley, and early return of service should be emphasized. Clay-court players should concentrate on groundstrokes, and will want to perfect such weapons as the loop and the drop shot.

GRIPS AND STROKES

Stroking reminders. Naturally, we try to develop the correct grips and strokes because these help us to achieve maximum control and power. Develop machinelike consistency in form, so that there is no variance from stroke to stroke. On groundstrokes and volleys, take your racket back quickly, so that you can stroke unhurriedly and smoothly. For better balance and leverage, bend your knees on waist-high and lower balls. Develop the habit of watching the ball carefully as it leaves your opponent's racket and comes toward your own. (In the middle of a match, do not suddenly try to watch the ball go into the strings of your own racket, unless you have done this before, since it can do you more harm than good.) Make sure you have either transferred your weight from back foot to front, in the direction the ball is going, or coiled and then uncoiled while making your stroke. Turn your shoulders as you hit each ball, since this motion is one of your primary sources of power.

Grip changes. Although it is relatively easy for the novice to learn proper techniques, it is extremely difficult to unlearn improper grips and strokes once they become grooved. Therefore, before attempting a drastic change, be sure you completely understand the consequences involved. Grip changes have caused many players considerable frustration and left them with shots inferior to those previously developed. Some of the factors to consider when making a drastic change are age, tennis experience, aspirations, and amount of practice time available. If you are able to play only once a week, try to shy away from any major grip change.

Fully understand grips. Most grips, regardless of how correct they may be, have disadvantages as well as advantages. It is important to understand what your grip can and cannot do for you. For example, if you use an extreme backhand grip, with thumb braced on the handle *(Fig. 1.2)*, and you also use a Western forehand (frying-pan) grip *(Fig. 1.3)*—neither of which is recommended—you should know that it takes a relatively long period of time to switch from forehand to backhand: on a fast exchange you will occasionally get caught in between the two grips. These grips are also poor for low balls, and they make slicing shots very difficult. However, you should understand that these extreme grips can be useful when a player wants to generate topspin.

Fig. 1.2 Extreme Eastern-backhand grip. This is not recommended.

Fig. 1.3 Western-forehand grip. This grip has many disadvantages.

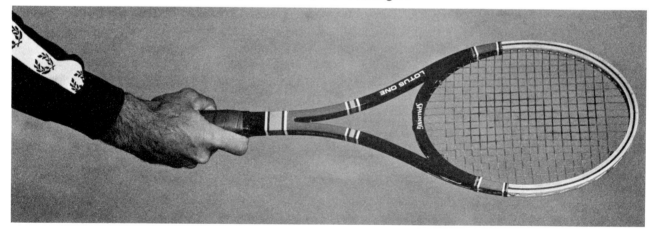

THE PRACTICE PROCEDURES YOU USE TODAY DETERMINE WHAT YOUR TENNIS GAME WILL BE LIKE TOMORROW

Correct grips and strokes, combined with intelligent and thoughtful practice procedures, are necessary ingredients to rapid improvement. When I see a person allowing a ball to bounce twice before hitting it when practicing today, I know that person is not going to be extraordinarily quick on a court next year. When an individual plays only once a week this year, I know there cannot be significant improvement, and he or she will be just a fair player next year. When I see a person easily beating all of his practice opponents this year, I know that player will not be ready for tough tournaments in the future. Without formidable competition, improvement is very difficult.

KEEP A TENNIS DIARY

Let us make no mistake about it: the road to tennis improvement can be a long and sometimes difficult one. Discouragement can occur, since progress is often slow and difficult to measure. The progress of a runner or swimmer can be easily gauged by a stopwatch. The pole-vaulter and javelin thrower knew the exact results of a performance with the use of a tape. Not so with the tennis player. He attempts to analyze improvement by noticing comparative scores against his opponents.

By not recording his results, the tennis player too often forgets his scores as the months go by and loses the few opportunities he has to receive feedback on his performance. For example, if you played Frank Jones in a practice or tournament match a year and a half ago, and you played him again today, it is important to be able to make a comparison of scores. Most often, assuming we are working hard on our games, we will receive a boost, or positive reinforcement, in knowing that we are progressing in tennis ability.

When coaching aspiring players whom I cannot see every day, I will require that they keep an accurate diary of their tennis activities. In this way I am able to check their tennis routines, and can advise them accordingly.

What should a diary consist of? It should simply have the date of the match, the opponent's name, the score, and whether the contest is practice or a tournament. If possible, a note or two should be made about the match itself. If you tried something and it worked, or it did not work, this information should be written down. If you drill, rather than play sets, the diary should indicate this along with the name of the person you drilled with. The total amount of time involved in the drilling should also be listed (*Fig. 1.4*).

TENNIS DIARY

Fig. 1.4 Keeping a tennis diary.

Notice of players:

Two rounds of doubles will be played starting at 4:30 PM

WEATHER

Temperature 93° ———
Humidity 91%

A tennis diary can also record scores made on a backboard. An accurate analysis of individual shot ability can be made, providing the player uses the same backboard and target, and stands the same distance from the wall. For example, standing behind a twenty-five-foot restraining line and limiting himself to two minutes, the player hits as many overspin-backhand drives as possible into a one-square-yard area. If a player was averaging fifteen last month, and twenty this month, he might be greatly motivated to continue to seek mastery of the game.

Besides serving as a barometer to judge our progress, a tennis diary can serve other functions. In some areas of the country, in order to be considered for a ranking, complete results of the previous year's tournament play must be turned in. To qualify for national events, a player often has to list all of his results. Also, it is a good idea to know whom you have beaten, for your own future reference. It is one good way to settle arguments about who won a given match. Some years ago there was a good-hearted but forgetful competitor who told a few people that he had beaten me regularly. With my having kept an up-to-date diary, this was quickly disproved. Maintaining a diary gives a player a realistic picture of his game. When a player becomes mentally "down" regarding his own progress, he can receive an extra boost by looking at his documented accomplishments. In the case of a player having delusions of grandeur about his accomplishments, the tennis diary can settle him gently back to earth.

If you have serious aspirations to improve, make sure that you have laid the kind of foundation upon which you can build a solid game. Only after establishing a firm technical base for your own tennis game should you begin utilizing different strategies and observing your opponent's characteristics. Understanding the opponent's weaknesses is the next step toward winning-tennis strategy.

Chapter 2

SCOUTING YOUR OPPONENT

WHAT IS SCOUTING?

In competitive athletics the term "scouting" means obtaining a preliminary view of an opponent before the actual encounter or contest takes place. Scouting can be done by the player himself, or by a coach, friend, or acquaintance who can submit a report. The more frequently an opponent is seen, the more precise is the picture of what to expect.

WHY SCOUT?

By having an accurate idea of what to expect from a tennis opponent, you do not have to waste points in the beginning of a match, attempting to figure out his strengths and weaknesses. If you know what resources he has or does not have before the start of a match, a solid game plan can be devised. For example, if you know he has an excellent backhand return of the American-twist service, you do not have to waste four or five points by serving to his backhand. Besides giving you an analysis of strokes, scouting tells you something about an opponent's temperament and his physical condition. He becomes more predictable, and in turn you attain greater calmness and objectivity.

WHEN SHOULD WE SCOUT?

Since scouting can be time-consuming, you should scout those players who are in your class or above it. It is a waste of time to watch a distinctly inferior player; more important things can be accomplished by you on or off the court.

Scouting is especially valuable if you are a flexible player who can vary your game according to the weaknesses of an opponent. You are less likely to profit by scouting if you play off your own strengths and use the same basic pattern of play in every match. As an amateur, the great Jack Kramer had such a style. He stroked his forehands, with sidespin, exclusively down the line, regardless of his opponent's ability.

DANGERS AND SHORTCOMINGS OF SCOUTING

Although you can easily observe a future opponent's tactics and strengths, you never know for sure how he will react to *your* style. The shock of being misled by a scouting report can be greater than that of coming into a match without information on an opponent.

A tendency when scouting an opponent is to view him in awe instead of as an ordinary human being who has certain frailties in his tennis game. Whenever you start investing an opponent with superhuman qualities, just remember the expression "He puts his pants on one foot at a time!"

HOW SHOULD WE SCOUT?

When scouting, if possible, sit behind one of the baselines, since it is here that you receive a much better idea of the strategy being used. Attempt to watch at least four or five games; otherwise, you receive an insufficient sampling of shots and draw conclusions based on invalid evidence. After playing the match with the opponent you scouted, make a few postmatch remarks on the report, and file it for future reference.

SCOUTING REPORT

The following are the basic ingredients of a tennis scouting report.

1. Serve

Direction. Where does he hit his aces? Can he hit *both* corners? Does he serve directly at the receiver?

Pace. Does he serve with speed and spin? [His speed without spin means depth, and makes it difficult for you to attack his second serve.] Will his second serve allow you enough time to run around your weaker side and hit your strongest shot?

Spin. Does he use any spins on service? If he has a twist service, does it kick high and invite an early return? Does he "telegraph" his intentions to slice or twist with the toss?

Depth. Does he have consistent depth on first and second service? [If he has depth, you should receive service farther back from the net.]

2. Forehand Groundstroke

High and Low Balls. How well does he handle these?

Number of Errors. What are the number of errors he makes on the forehand compared with the backhand?

Direction. Where does he usually hit his putaway forehands? Does he vary the direction of his passing shots, or does he tend to hit only crosscourt or only down the line?

Depth and Pace. Does he have consistency and power on his forehand?

Takes Balls Early or Late. Does he stand in dangerously close and try to take the ball very early on groundstrokes? (If so, attempt to hit very deep to extract an error or a mishit ball.) Does he hit too late on passing shots?

3. Backhand Groundstroke

High and Low Balls. Does he have trouble with a high-bouncing, slow-paced ball? Can he slice a short and low ball?

Number of Errors. Is his backhand steadier than his forehand?

Overspin. Can he hit overspin passing shots?

Direction. Where does he hit most of his backhand passing shots?

Depth and Pace. Can he hit consistently deep and hard off the backhand?

Takes Balls Early or Late. Is there any kind of a hesitation (allowing the ball to drop too low) on his passing shots?

4. Volley

Positioning. Does he volley while standing close to the net or does he stand back around the service line? (In the former case he is likely to be vulnerable to the lob, whereas in the latter situation he might have difficulty with the slow dink to his feet. Closing in quickly is one sign of a fine volleyer.)

Low Volleys. Does he try to hit them too hard? [Jimmy Connors has a weakness on low backhand volleys, which he hits two-handed, but most players cannot take advantage of it because of his super approach shots.]

Forehand or Backhand Strength. Is one of his volleys noticeably weaker than the other?

Direction. Is his putaway volley usually hit in one direction?

Pace. How does he react to a very hard or very soft ball?

5. Overhead

Pace. Does he put away his overheads on a clay court, or can you run them down and keep the ball in play?

Direction. Where does he aim most of his smashes?

6. Return of Service

Direction. When served to his backhand or his forehand side in either of the service boxes, does he have a tendency to return the ball consistently in one direction?

Net Clearance. Can he accurately hit a low return of service?

Pace. Can he hit hard, and accurately, on his backhand return of service?

Ability to Attack a Second Service. Does he clobber a slow second service?

Receiving Twist. Has he had experience returning a twist? Can he take it early?

Forehand vs. Backhand Ability. Which return-of-service wing is his most reliable considering accuracy and power?

Positioning. Where does he stand to receive service?

7. Lob

Accuracy of Forehand and Backhand. Does he have one side or the other that offers little threat of an accurate lob?

Frequency of Lob. Does he lob frequently, periodically, or seldom?

8. Drop Shot

Threat. Can he hit an accurate drop shot off both forehand and backhand?

When Is He Most Likely to Drop-shot? Does he drop-shot only short and slow balls, or can he accurately hit one from the baseline?

Backswing. Does he reveal his intent to drop-shot by taking a particular kind of backswing on his stroke?

9. Stamina

In Comparison with You. Are you in better condition than he?

Rate of Stamina Loss. Does his game deteriorate fast when he is tired?

Analysis of Overweight Condition. Although he is overweight, are you sure he is in poor condition?

10. Speed and Reflexes

Afoot. Does your opponent have great running speed, average speed, or is he slow?

Hands. Does he react quickly to balls served or hit directly at him?

11. Size

Forecourt Vulnerability. Is he short enough so that if drawn to the net he could be lobbed or passed?

High Ball Weakness. Is he susceptible to a high-bouncing groundstroke loop or a twist service? [If he is short, he usually will have difficulty with high balls.]

Knowing what an opponent can and cannot do on a tennis court is essential to applying good strategy. If you are unconcerned with your opponent's attributes, and simply play your own game, you will not be as effective as you should be.

In order to be able to handle an adversary we must develop certain strengths and assets ourselves. There are preparations we can make to enable us to be effective against any opponent. These preparations are necessary to carry out a tennis battle plan.

Chapter 3

MATCH-PREPARATION TACTICS

This chapter deals with measures a player can take to prepare for an upcoming tennis tournament.

PHYSICAL CONDITIONING

The first factor to think about is your physical fitness. There are many U.S. tournaments for males that require a person to play as many as three singles matches, plus a doubles match or two, in one day *(Fig. 3.1)*. The best method of preparing for such a tournament is to schedule two tough singles matches (three or four sets each) in a day, and supplement this with a physical conditioning program.

WEST SQEEDUNK CLAY COURT TENNIS TOURNAMENT

SINGLES AND DOUBLES

AUGUST 8–9

SATURDAY SCHEDULE (TOP HALF)

	9:00	12:00	3:00
Barker	___		
Sherman		___	
Walker	___		___
Kileff		___	
Lucas	___		
Schoenlank		___	
Tully			___
Oldham		___	

Notice of players:

Two rounds of doubles will be played starting at 4:30 PM

WEATHER

Temperature 93° ———
Humidity 91%

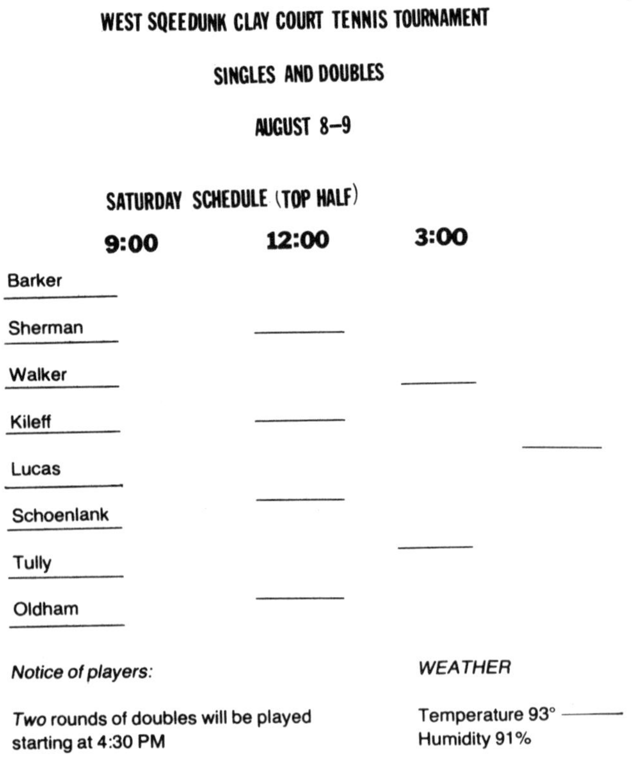

Fig. 3.1 Be in top condition if you have aspirations of winning West Squeedunk.

Regardless of the style of game you play, when the temperature is above 90 degrees on a slow clay court, it is impossible to win against a steady player unless you are fit. It is an ominous sign for the unfit player when he and his opponent break into a sweat before even walking on the court.

An excellent way to supplement the conditioning benefits derived from drilling and the playing of practice sets is to run distances and to do a few wind sprints. In addition to promoting good physical condition, running helps make a player psychologically tough. When a player can endure a thirty-minute run, his fears of facing a grueling match are lessened.

Off-court conditioning. Let me offer a word of caution regarding off-court physical-conditioning programs. Hard training methods such as performing tough exercises, running, and lifting weights are not particularly palatable compared with playing the game itself. If you overindulge in these kinds of activities, you can become turned off to your whole tennis-improvement project. When planning a three- or four-year tennis-development program, you should be aware of the fact that to maintain your interest and motivation, rewards must be plentiful, and unpleasantries kept to a minimum. Since financial rewards are light years away from the beginning player, this has to be discounted as a legitimate motivating force. (Neither you nor I nor Jimmy Connors nor Bjorn Borg will ever get paid while *learning* the basic rudiments of tennis.) Doing 30 kangaroo jumps and 50 pushups each night is fine, provided you can tolerate the discomfort. If not, you should restrict your tennis activities to more pleasurable on-court pursuits.

PRACTICE AGAINST TOUGH COMPETITION AND IN VARYING CONDITIONS

Although it is wise to practice occasionally with

those you can beat, it is important to meet plenty of players who can defeat you and force you to your mental and physical limits. Tournament players are tougher than nontournament and unranked players since they are more tenacious, and are usually steadier, faster, and hit with better pace and depth.

Take precautions to schedule a variety of opponents so that you can quickly apply the appropriate strategy when meeting diverse stylists in tournaments. Unless you practice with such players as the big-serving cat who comes in on every ball, or the fast and steady pusher who does not miss, you will probably not be able to cope with them adequately in a tournament.

Since there will be some stylists whom you will be unable to schedule in practice, it is important that you use your weapons in a variety of ways against whomever you practice with. For example, although you might not have a good left-hander to play at your local courts, you can still direct all of your balls to a right-hander's forehand throughout a set or two of practice. This stimulates the general procedure used against most southpaws. It is also advisable to use differing tactics, such as groundstroking from the back of the court, looping, and trying drop shots and lobs.

Playing matches away from your local club or park is excellent match-preparation strategy, because by doing so you become accustomed to varying conditions. By traveling to different courts for practice action, you are forced to play on fast and slow surfaces with a variety of ball bounces. Wind conditions, background, shadows, and type of court-boundary lines can vary markedly from one court complex to another. Some tennis centers have disturbing elements, such as the courts' being placed too close together, resulting in balls rolling on to your court about every second or third point. At other clubs you will have continuous loud talking, or inexperienced spectators or players walking near you during the middle of a rally. In order to be a complete player, you should learn to cope with unpredictable situations by experiencing them in practice. If you have encountered these unusual conditions enough times in the past, you can play a somewhat normal game despite them.

When you are scheduled for a tournament match only a couple of days away, try to play on courts that are similar to the one you will be using in the competition. Very often this is not feasible, so, if you possibly can, play on faster courts than those to be used in the tournament. Going from fast to slow courts is usually much easier than going from slow to fast.

TRY TO LIVE A RELAXED LIFE

When you are playing tournaments, it is important that you try to live as relaxed a life as possible. You should not be burdened with deadlines and tensions. To function well on a court, a player must be free to concentrate on the game itself, and not be burdened with professional or personal problems. If this is impossible, then do not expect breathtaking results.

Establishing a pattern of regularity in sleeping hours is important. Whether you go to bed at 10 P.M. or A.M. does not matter; the crucial factor is that you do it on a steady basis and have at least seven and a half or eight hours of sleep each day.

I do not advocate living a Spartan type of life, since it can be tension-producing. The small amount that one has to gain by living a monk's existence off the court (extremely careful diet, etc.) can be costly in the long run. You have sacrificed enough *on* the court; *off* the court, indulge in activities that you enjoy. Remember, the important prerequisite for tennis success is to structure an intelligent on-court tennis program, and work hard at it.

TRY TO GAIN AN ADVANTAGE IN EQUIPMENT

Having proper tennis equipment not only helps assure you of producing your best tennis game but affords you the least amount of mental and physical discomfort.

For the aspiring player, having at least two matching rackets is essential. By matching, I mean using the identical brand from a racket manufacturer. Not only the grip size and weight but also the balance point (*Fig. 3.2*) should be the same. Finding matching rackets is much easier with metal or synthetic rackets than with wood. With the latter you are fortunate when you can obtain rackets that vary less than one quarter ounce in total weight and whose balance points are less than one quarter of an inch apart. If possible, the string pressure in all of your rackets should be similar. Before playing a tournament match, make sure the strings in at least two of your rackets are in excellent shape, not fraying or dead.

There are two tidbits of advice that should be passed on about the purchase of rackets. First, when you are shopping for a racket and are unsure about the weight and balance you prefer, select one that is light in the head. You can always *add* a little bit of weight to the top of a racket with tape, but you cannot

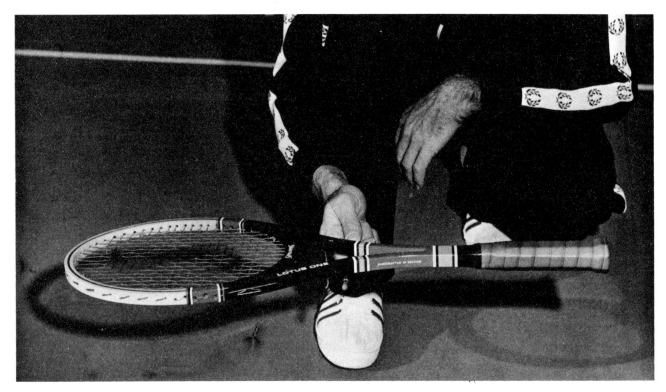

Fig. 3.2 Finding the balance point of a racket.

successfully reduce the weight of a racket without weakening it. Second, when purchasing a wood racket, make sure it is not warped; place it on a table and notice the distance between the throat and table; then turn it over and observe whether the other side is the same (*Fig. 3.3*). Remember, a press can prevent a wood racket from warping, but it cannot straighten one out.

Equally as important as having proper rackets is the use of proper tennis shoes. Your shoes should fit comfortably, and, if you will be playing on slippery clay, you should have deep grooves in the soles, to gain decent traction. This is especially important for a tall person. A heavy tennis shoe can be to your advantage on clay, because it tends to dig into the ground a little more, whereas lightness is desirable for hard-court matches. When practicing on hard courts, however, use the new type tennis shoes with leather uppers if you come down heavily on your feet, since these help absorb the impact of the uncushioned surface.

DAY-OF-THE-MATCH REMINDERS

Develop game plans. Before walking on the court you should develop a tactical plan to use against your opponent. One such tactic might be as follows: if he has no backhand at all and your volley is exceptional, go to the net behind every ball that goes to his backhand. You should also be contemplating your service direction, overhead direction, pace, and whether you want to shorten or lengthen points.

We develop game plans from various sources of information. These include our past observations of the player, what we might have heard about him, or even our observations of him in the warmup. Occasionally, we start a match with the simple intention of playing our normal and most comfortable game. Then, as the match progresses, we can develop a slightly different plan based on our observations of the types of shots that are extracting the most errors. It is best to have a game plan fixed well in mind beforehand, regardless

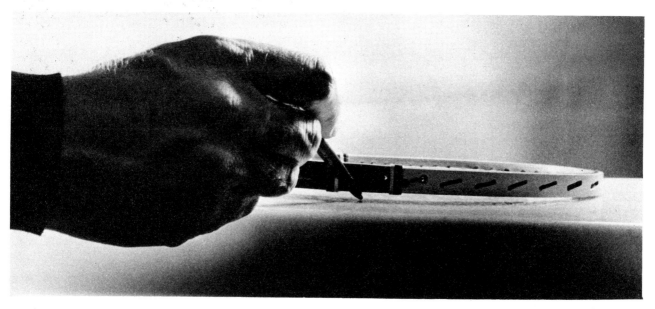

Fig. 3.3 Checking for a warp in the racket. Measure the distance between the table and the head of the racket; then turn the racket over and do the same on the other side.

of how simple the plan is. This is called the "primary game plan."

In addition to knowing your primary game plan before walking on the court, you should have at least one alternative plan in case the first fails. This emergency plan is called the "secondary game plan" and consists of a set of tactics slightly different from the primary game plan. The object of game plans is, first, to enable you to do your thinking outside of the heat of battle and, second, to make you firmer in your convictions and your actions on the court. Doubt is an enemy of the wise tactical player.

Warm up early, for relaxation and timing. Relaxation while playing is important, since it conserves energy and helps us maintain control over the delicate body movements required in advanced tennis. There are measures that should be taken to keep nervousness to a minimum. A thirty- to forty-five-minute warmup early on the day of the match can loosen a person up without causing him fatigue. When scheduled to play a clay-court match, warming up on a backboard can be very beneficial. If a person is very inexperienced, a longer and more strenuous hit of an hour and a half to two hours might be wise. If it comes to a choice between a long and a short warmup, it is better to go into a match a *little* tired than *very* nervous. Inci-

dentally, there are a few circuit players who prefer to jog or exercise on the day of a match.

An early warmup is especially important in certain conditions such as a singles match on a fast surface, or a doubles match on any surface, since a person can lose the contest by playing just a couple of bad points. Being thoroughly warmed up is also important for big hitters whose shots demand greater precision and muscle control. Those of us with short, slow strokes have the advantage of being less prone to off days caused by improper timing and nervousness. However, the author is not advocating this consistent and soft stroking style for those with extremely high tennis ambitions.

An early warmup on the day of a match is not always advisable. On extremely hot days, when playing on slow courts, stamina becomes a vital issue. For certain players, including older competitors, a one-hour warmup can put them right out of a match.

If you do warm up, take precautions not to linger in the hot sun when you're finished, since this can be unnoticeably tiring. Also, try not to watch any tennis for two or three hours before your match; this can tire your eyes and weaken your concentration.

A *little* bit of nervousness and anxiety is helpful because it protects you from forgetting about the importance of the matter at hand. If you have some apprehension, you will be less inclined to play a loose stroke on an important point during a tournament match.

BEFORE YOU WALK ON THE COURT: A CHECKLIST

Before starting any tournament, ascertain what the policy is for allowing new balls for the third set. (In the final rounds of smaller tournaments, and throughout major events, there is usually a change of balls after a specified number of games.) If you are expecting any difficulty at all from your opponent, bring water, juice, or another thirst-quenching sports beverage with you if it is not available on the court. Make sure you have good laces in your tennis shoes. In addition, bring at least one or two towels; have tape, in case you develop a blister; and take an extra pair of socks. If you perspire freely, make sure you wear a sweatband on your wrist, even perhaps across your forehead. When playing in a wooded area that has bugs and mosquitoes, bring insect repellent to the courts and apply it as needed. This will aid you in maintaining good concentration without having to contend with insect bites. If the temperature is at all chilly, have a sweat suit with you so your muscles will not stiffen. Loose-fitting clothes (preferably with pockets, to hold balls) can help to make your court stay a comfortable one.

The use of "favorite" or newer clothing and equipment during an important match can often give a player a valuable psychological lift. In practice, try to wear that pair of shoes that lacks some traction, or wear a shirt that does not quite feel right, or use your "second" racket that has the strings whose tension may

Fig. 3.4 Singles sticks are used in major tournaments. The sticks are 3'6" high, and placed three feet outside the singles sidelines.

have slipped a fraction. Entering a tournament with the conviction your match equipment is slightly better than that used in practice is a positive psychological maneuver.

If you are playing on a clay court, and the court is extremely dry, it is your privilege to ask that the court be watered. A slippery clay court can be a safety hazard, and, in addition, the tennis will not be as good as it should be. If the court is in reasonably good shape, such a request can be viewed, perhaps rightfully so, with amused suspicion; it could be interpreted as an attempt by a steady player to gain a slight advantage over a hard hitter.

Years ago, on the European tennis circuit, there was an incredibly steady, and also humorous, player by the name of William Alvarez, of Colombia, South America. Before some of his matches on clay, in which he invariably faced a harder hitter, he would take measures to slow down the speed of the court. Alvarez would either give the groundskeeper a generous tip to drench the court with water or have a friend sprinkle it liberally. The court would be slowed down to such an extent that even Ellsworth Vines, the hardest hitter in history, would have difficulty putting the ball away! The ball would pick up so much moisture it would resemble the shot-putter's shot. Under these conditions Alvarez was competitive with almost everyone. This was just one of many ploys he would use. Although they disliked opposing him, the boys on the circuit looked forward with glee to Alvarez's tricks.

In tournaments, singles sticks should be used on all courts with doubles-alley markings, in order to give the net its proper height at the sidelines (Fig. 3.4). If sticks are not being used, it would be considered improper for you to bring them out only for your own matches. You should use singles sticks in practice matches if they are available where you are working out.

Before starting a match, you should measure the net to insure its proper height. Measuring the net in the *middle* of a match was another of William Alvarez's favorite stall-and-psych tactics. He often resorted to this questionable practice when his opponent had momentum and had just hit a let-cord winner.

Finally, let me mention that if you are ever given the choice of when you would like to schedule your match with a big server, by all means arrange for it to be played during the middle of the day, when you have maximum light. Having to play such a contest in the late-afternoon hours can sometimes result in an unwarranted loss because you cannot see the opponent's serve well enough. Although it is usually beyond our control, it is best that we play against hard hitters on shadowless courts.

In this chapter we have dealt with the long- and short-term preparations for a tennis match. The match is now about to be played, and our opponent is dressed and waiting at the referee's desk to be assigned a court.

Chapter 4

HOW TO WARM UP FOR A MATCH

Before going out to the court and starting your warmup, make sure you "try" to use the toilet. There is nothing more disconcerting than having your court concentration broken by a biological urge that could have been taken care of at the proper time.

DETERMINING SIDE OR SERVICE

When you and your opponent reach the court, spin a racket to determine who starts serving or receiving, and which player chooses the starting side. This is the accepted routine followed by tournament players; do not warm up and *then* decide service or side.

When two good players meet on a fast court such as grass or cement, it is often psychologically advantageous for the player with first choice to serve first. In this way, providing both are winning their service games, the player who received service during the first game is spending much of the time one game behind his serving opponent (0–1, 1–2, 2–3, 3–4, etc.). The pressure is usually on the player who served second, since he must hold service to stay even.

On the other hand, there are some players who feel they serve better in the second game of a match than they would during the first game, and thus prefer to receive service to start the first set. Another category of players prefer to receive service initially, knowing their opponents are slow in developing a good rhythm in the first game of a match. They hope to break service early. In a match in which many breaks of service are anticipated, as a match between two soft servers, the result of the match choice to determine side or service has little or no significance.

HOW VIGOROUS SHOULD THE WARMUP BE?

Those who have a history of elbow, wrist, or shoulder trouble are best off swinging the racket for a minute or two without hitting the ball. Simulate ground-strokes and service. Shoulder injuries can be minimized if a player hangs by the hands (palms away) from the open door of a tennis-fence gate or the branch of a tree before he starts hitting. Unless you have been vigorously warming up on a nearby court with someone else, move and swing slowly during the first few minutes of the actual warmup. If you are wearing a sweater or warmup suit, take it off only after you break a sweat or begin to feel loose.

As your muscles gradually stretch, move a little faster to retrieve balls hit by your opponent. Pick up the pace or speed of your ball so that it will equal that used in the match. The inexperienced or nervous player should use the second half of the warmup to work hard and get the "nervous edge" off.

DETERMINING THE LENGTH OF THE WARMUP

A few tournaments will request that you limit the warmup to ten minutes, or, in a very few cases, to five minutes. In the majority of tournament matches, however, players are allowed some flexibility in setting their own warmup length. In the latter situation, pay particular attention to the physical condition of your opponent, and make a comparison with your own stamina and strength. If you appear to have a definite edge in this department, do not be reluctant to lengthen the "knockup." You do this by simply allowing your opponent to take the initiative in moving through the various phases of the warmup. Conversely, if you are the person who is lacking stamina, be sure not to spend extra time warming up.

Both of these ploys are quite ethical, providing you do not go directly against the wishes of your opponent. You should never delay a warmup after ten or fifteen minutes if your opponent has asked that the match commence.

PLACEMENT OF SHOTS IN THE WARMUP

Speaking of ethics, during the warmup you must aim your balls directly at your opponent, so that rallies can be maintained. When he is in the back of the court, place your shots as deep as possible, whether you are on the opposite baseline or volleying from your forecourt. When your opponent is near the net, keep your groundstrokes as low as possible and take the balls as quickly as you can. In carefully aiming your balls, you are, in reality, using the warmup as a valuable practice period. When practicing service, aim your balls to the corners of the service box.

ACCENTUATE PROPER OR NORMAL MATCH FORM IN WARMUP

You must take precautions to use proper and careful stroking form when warming up for a tennis match. During this period you should avoid the tendency to become sloppy, even though points are not being counted. You should use this opportunity further to develop correct strokes and footwork. For example, if on most backhand volleys in a match you step forward with the right foot, you should not use an open stance in the warmup.

WHAT SHOULD A WARMUP CONSIST OF, AND WHAT IS THE NORMAL TIME ALLOTMENT FOR EACH STROKE?

The warmup should include all of the main shots you intend to use in a match. We usually do not practice stop volleys or drop shots, but if we do this, we would certainly limit each to only two or three shots.

There is an accepted approximate warmup time for each of the strokes; however, this can be changed if both partners agree to alter the format. For example, if one player wants to warm up by just practicing lobs, and his opponent wants to practice only overhead smashes, it would be perfectly acceptable for them to engage in this unusual practice. Such an agreement would probably result in some belly laughs by specta-tors, but since its occurrence is highly unlikely, let us discuss normal time allotments for strokes in a ten-minute warmup. The following is a rough guide that most tournament players adhere to:

Groundstrokes. Usually are hit for five or six minutes, but occasionally are practiced longer.

Serves. Ten to twenty serves is considered proper. If a player needs a longer service-warmup period he should practice with someone else before his opponent arrives to play. Since tennis rules require "continuous" play, all practice serves by *both* players must be taken before the first point of the match is played.

Volleys. Two to four minutes. It would not be considered proper to volley eight to ten minutes of a warmup.

Overheads. Six to fifteen smashes is the accepted number.

Return of Service. Although most serves are caught and served back, occasionally practicing the return of service is proper and acceptable.

ADDITIONAL WARMUP SUGGESTIONS

If you are playing your match on an unfamiliar surface or on one you have not competed on for a considerable length of time, hit as many groundstrokes as possible. Whenever you move from a slower to a faster surface, make a concerted effort to get your racket back fast as the ball is approaching.

If you intend to serve and volley in the match itself, be sure to run toward the net after a few practice serves, to gain better timing.

To attain greater concentration on the ball during the match, try watching it intently in the warmup. By observing the seams and rotation of the ball, you will probably become more relaxed and less self-conscious than if you allow your mind to drift. Making a deliberate effort to watch the ball in the warmup is important. Sizing up your opponent is equally essential to the use of intelligent tactics in the match.

Chapter 5

OBSERVING YOUR OPPONENT DURING THE WARMUP, TO DETERMINE TACTICS

WHAT A WARMUP DOES NOT REVEAL

At the outset of this brief chapter it should be stated that there are some strengths and weaknesses in an opponent's game that you will not see as you warm up with him. You cannot observe uncanny steadiness pertaining to ball placement near lines, since shots are directed down the middle of the court during the warmup. You can be grossly deceived by an opposing player who is lazy and does not concentrate on his prematch shots (there are a number of these). A few players will hit softer or harder in the warmup than they will in a match. Tenacity, lasting power, can only be seen with surety in the match itself. We can tell more about an opponent's *overall ability* in one or two games, which take only five or six minutes to play, than we can from a twenty-five-minute warmup with him. Nevertheless, a warmup can offer valuable cues regarding the specific assets of an opponent.

OPPONENT'S PHYSICAL CONDITION

Observe your opponent and see if he appears to be in good physical condition. Is he muscled or unmuscled; is he overweight or trim? By looking at his body you can get a clue as to his stamina. Naturally, when faced with a good-stroking but out-of-condition opponent, we try to lengthen points and to keep him out on the court as long as possible. This matter of exploiting opponents' physical weaknesses will be dealt with in more detail in subsequent chapters.

WHAT OBSERVATIONS SHOULD YOU MAKE AS YOUR OPPONENT STROKES THE BALL?

Gross errors. Make a mental note whenever your opponent makes a glaring error during the warmup. If he hits the bottom of the net or the fence, for example, with a forehand volley, remember this error. Although it might mean very little, it could indicate a stroke that is very shaky.

Late hitting. Are there any shots your opponent delays? He might have a hitch or a momentary pause in a stroke. Does he have any strokes that he takes slightly behind him, or does he delay a particular shot by stepping back just before hitting it? For example, if he hesitates before hitting his backhand groundstroke, you should look for the chance to come to the net against him. In this case you would have the opportunity to close in tight at the net, and intercept his attempted passing shots.

Clues on groundstrokes. In an attempt to find out which of his groundstrokes is the weakest, make a rough tabulation of his errors off the forehand compared with those off the backhand. His pace off one wing compared with that off the other will be obvious. Try to ascertain with which stroke he is able to "keep the ball on the strings" for the longest period of time. This is somewhat difficult for the unpracticed eye to determine.

Is he able to drive and slice with both the forehand and backhand groundstrokes? If he cannot slice, he will likely have trouble handling balls landing short in his court (*Fig. 5.1*). He might be vulnerable to a net attack if he cannot hit hard. Conversely, if he is a power hitter, it is likely his passing shots will be effective.

Fig. 5.1 Backhand slice. If your opponent cannot slice his backhand (as above), he will have difficulty handling a short, low ball.

As you are warming up, notice if your opponent has the ability and inclination to hit soft as well as hard balls. Hard hitters are occasionally going to miss, and if they cannot temporize or slow down their swing, they can give away points (and matches) very quickly.

Clues on opponents's volley and overhead. Just as you make a comparison between a player's forehand and backhand groundstrokes, you should also do this on his forehand and backhand volley. Is one hit later, or with less accuracy and pace, than the other? Often a player's best volley will be on the same side as his most effective groundstroke.

When making observations of your opponent's volley during the warmup, watch where he stands in the court as he practices them. Frequently, a player will volley in a match from about the same place where he stands in practice. Naturally, if he stands close to the net, he will be vulnerable to the lob; and if he volleys

from near the service line, he will have considerable difficulty with low, dipping balls or dinks landing near his feet.

A player can possess a great volley, but if he does not have a decent smash, you can nullify his net attack by lobbing. As you watch him hit his overhead smash, notice if he is hitting the ball in the center of his strings. Also observe his athletic ability to see if he leaps well, to cover your quick, low-trajectory lobs. You can notice the pace of his smashes, knowing that if he cannot hit the ball with speed, you will be able to run down almost all of his overheads. Finally, look at his smashing action and see if he is taking a full windup instead of a half swing. The player who uses the full swing on the overhead will have considerable power, but will suffer greatly in terms of accuracy.

Observe opponent's service during the warmup. Watch your opponent's ball toss in order to pick up a clue regarding the kind of serve he will be hitting (slice, flat, or twist). Observe the depth of his serves to be able to make a judgment on how close you can safely receive them. Since some players will give you only a minimum number of their most effective serves in the warmup, be ready to adjust to tougher serves once the match begins.

OTHER IMPORTANT WARMUP OBSERVATIONS

Left- or right-hander. Look for this quickly in the warmup. Experienced tournament players will notice immediately whether they are playing a left-hander. Inexperienced players will often play a whole match not knowing whether they're playing a left- or right-hander.

Two-handed backhand. A player who uses this grip will have difficulty handling short, low and wide balls hit to his two-handed side. His passing shots will often be devastating, since they can be hit hard, and placement is well disguised.

Two Forehands. Hitting with two forehands gives a player considerable range and reach. Nevertheless, hitting with either hand is an undesirable practice because you have to change hands when volleying. Usually the backhand volley is vulnerable because it gets no practice, since groundstrokes are made with only forehands. Two-handers are weakest when the action becomes faster, as they are forced to make a quick switch from hand to hand.

You have completed the warmup, and the match is about to begin. You will start with baseline play, since the majority of points of most tennis matches are played with both opponents in positions near their baselines.

Chapter 6

BASELINE TACTICS

GENERAL PRINCIPLES OF BASELINE PLAY

Keep the ball in play. The outcome of the vast majority of tennis matches is decided not by your hitting winning placements and scorching aces, but by your committing fewer errors than your opponent. Minimizing mistakes is the backbone of a winning game. An affirmative answer to the following question indicates tenacious traits that have winning implications: "Are you willing to hit ten balls in every rally so that you will win two out of every three points played, rather than have brief three-ball rallies that end with your losing two out of every three points?" Many players do not have the patience to engage in lengthy rallies.

Attack only if the percentages of winning the point are in your favor. Ordinarily you should attack only short or soft balls (*Fig. 6.1*); be content the remainder of the time to prolong the rally and attempt to extract that short ball. Usually, it makes no sense to gamble by attacking if your opponent is in good position.

Fig. 6.1 Forehand putaway. With opponent out of position, a hard winning drive can be attempted.

Attacking shots should be made with caution. You must be careful not to use attacking and risky shots until you become accustomed to your opponent's rhythm. Since we often do not have good timing in the first or second game of a match, it is best to play the early games somewhat conservatively.

Although for some players it is good strategy to come to the net when given a soft short ball, for other players this would be unwise. The matter of whether or not you should attack a short ball is centered around the question, "Am I going to win the majority of points in which I do this?" You can lose many points if you do not have accurate forcing groundstrokes and a sound volley. Moving to the net can also be a losing proposition if your opponent happens to have formidable passing shots. Exercise discretion in deciding whether to sojourn to the net.

Keep the opponent moving. When an opponent has his feet firmly planted, he strokes in an unhurried manner, and will hit harder and more accurately than if hitting on the run. As ball placement is developed, we become more capable of keeping an opponent off balance by moving him around the court. Since a beginning player must be content to hit the ball near the center of his opponent's court, he will not have the skill to run his opponent hard. On the other hand, a tournament player can place his shots within five or six feet of the sideline and baseline, and thus can force an opponent to move.

One criterion we use to judge our opponent's level of play is his ability to jockey us about the court. The more we have to work, the better is the opposing player.

Use a variety of shots against an opponent. When you vary the speed and the spin on the ball, it is difficult for your opponent to develop rhythm and to stroke well. Combinations, such as two soft slices followed by a hard drive, can often extract an errant shot from your adversary. Tennis players, like baseball hitters, thrive on anticipating the type of ball they will receive.

The disadvantage of using variety is that in some cases it can upset the hitter more than the receiver. In addition, it prevents him from fully developing one particular shot. To be able to execute stroke combinations, a player must practice them, and, unfortunately, this is time-consuming. Let us suppose a player who has a medley of shots and ball speeds spends one third of his stroking time hitting loops, one third of his time hitting flat drives, and one third executing over-

spin drives. (The loop is stroked similarly to the low lob and is aimed high over the net, whereas the overspin drive has a three- or four-foot safety margin over the net.) This would be fine; however, if he did away with the flat drive and the loop, he would triple his practice time on the overspin drive.

Although many fine players use variety, there are a few others, equally effective, who hit in a very predictable and straightforward manner. (Don Budge was in the latter category—a great player with a powerful yet simplified game.) Thus, some variety in stroking is desirable, but care must be taken not to overdo it.

As a match progresses, gauge who is running the most. If you are working much harder than your opponent *and* losing the match, there is no question that you must change tactics. The dilemma comes when you are winning, yet laboring harder than he. In this case you should ask yourself, "Do I have enough strength to continue working this hard and close him out with a victory, or am I likely to run out of stamina after just a few more punishing games?" You must be able accurately to calculate your own energy reserves, and have an awareness of the speed with which you lose your physical resources. In order to know this endurance capacity, you must have been involved in exhausting encounters in the past.

In baseline rallies, where should you position yourself on the court? In most cases stand a yard or so behind your center mark. You should ordinarily make ball contact with a groundstroke about ten feet from where the ball bounces. Therefore, you should rarely be forced to retreat more than ten feet behind the baseline on the deepest possible shot hit by your opponent.

The more experienced you become, the quicker you will detect your opponent's stroke direction. Your anticipation of his shot placement should be based on his past stroking patterns and the way he lines up his body. Also, if you are forced off court, you should be cognizant of the fact that he will probably direct his ball to the obvious opening. In the instances when you have given your opponent a "sitter," and he is likely to blast your short ball away for a winner, take a step or two in the direction you think he is going to aim the ball to gain a quick start.

In instances when you are playing an opponent who has excellent groundstrokes, but is lacking a good net game, you can position yourself eight or ten feet from the baseline. When standing such a distance behind the baseline you will receive balls that have slowed down considerably. You will also allow yourself more time to retrieve hard-hit balls. Nevertheless, do not make a habit of playing points from far behind your baseline, since this style of game has little basis on which to develop.

When both you and your opponent are in the backcourt, and you hit a short low ball near one of his sidelines, if you can volley reasonably well, you should move to a position about two to three yards inside your baseline. By assuming this position, you are ready to volley any ball for a winner that he pops up from his awkward position (*Fig. 6.2*).

No-Man's-Land. In placing yourself between the baseline and service line you are in an area known as "no-man's-land." We usually do not position ourselves here; we stay either just behind the baseline or in the forecourt near the net. If we used "no-man's-land" as our regular home base we would have to contend with difficult balls landing near our feet. When his opponent is at the net, an expert and agile volleyer will occasionally step into "no-man's-land" in an attempt to wrest the forecourt position from him. In this instance "no-man's-land" might be more accurately termed "net-rusher's-land."

BE CONCERNED WITH DEPTH AND NET CLEARANCE.

Net clearance. If you are a beginner, aim your groundstrokes at least four or five feet above the net so that you allow a reasonable safety margin. (Also, aim down the center of the court until you can safely hit closer to the lines.) Maintaining sufficient height on balls will also help to achieve depth of shot.

Fig. 6.2   Stepping inside baseline and preparing to volley opponent's weak return.

Depth. Hitting consistently deep into the opponent's court is very effective. High-ranked international-tournament players usually stroke with excellent depth.

In the 1950s I witnessed a clay-court match between Jaroslav Drobny, the great Czech left-hander, and Gardnar Mulloy, a top U.S. player. It was a privately staged match (only about five of us were there) that took place at the Roney Plaza Hotel courts, in Miami Beach, Florida. There was no love lost between these two players. Although Mulloy was not an angel in tennis clothes, this particular day it was Drobny who was cantankerous. He was arguing about line calls as if there were $50,000 riding on the outcome. I was a baseline umpire and to this day I am still amazed at Drobny's depth of groundstoke. His overspin forehand was vicious. Most of his balls would land about five or six feet from the baseline. When he mishit slightly, the ball would land three or four feet, or seven or eight feet from the baseline. Drobny won the match, continuing his mastery of Mulloy. At his peak, Drobny was one of the three or four best players in the world.

The following are the main advantages of hitting with depth:

1. When you stroke with depth, it is difficult for your opponent to attack. (If he tries to come to the net after hitting a shot from behind his baseline, he lacks adequate time to move close enough to the net to execute a good volley.)
2. When you keep your opponent deep in his court, it is difficult for him to place his balls at a sharp angle (*Fig. 6.3*), where he can make outright putaways, and to run you hard.
3. When your opponent is hitting from behind his baseline, you have more time to gain good position while awaiting his return.
4. Since depth requires ample height over the net, it decreases a player's chances of erring into the barrier.
5. An opponent's drop-shot threat can almost be nullified when you force him to hit from behind his baseline. You will have too much time to reach the drop shot, so he rarely can use it.
6. When you hit deep to an opponent, he is allowed much less time to prepare for your shot. Assuming he is standing one yard behind his baseline, and your ball lands six inches inside it, he will probably be forced to take the ball as it is coming up from the ground. Hitting a ball on the rise is risky, and errors frequently occur. Provided it is

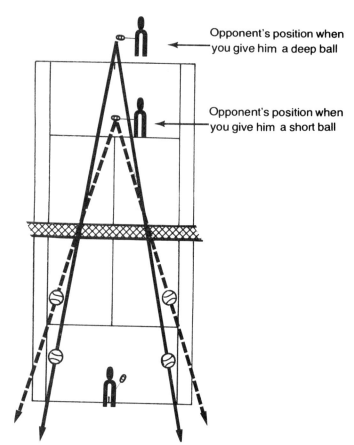

Opponent's position when you give him a deep ball

Opponent's position when you give him a short ball

Fig. 6.3   When opponent is moved farther from the net, his hitting angle is reduced.

not a lob, the farther a ball travels through the air to a given point, the faster it will arrive. Therefore, an opponent is rushed much more when you hit a ball that bounces close to his feet (*Fig. 6.4*).

Hitting low over the net. There are many times when players (especially beginners and intermediates) should deliberately give an opponent a short ball to hit instead of a deep one. When we intentionally hit short, we should lower our ball trajectory, clearing the net by just one or two feet. Some players have difficulty when presented with a short low ball to return. They might lack the skill to hit as they run forward, or they could have the tendency to overhit (using too much power, resulting in an error over the baseline or sidelines). One of the best plays against an outstanding looper is to hit *shallow*, forcing him to loop from *inside* his baseline, where he has the tendency to err over your baseline.

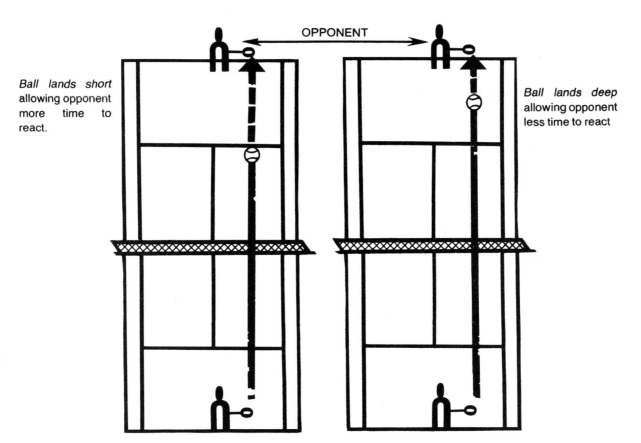

OPPONENT

Ball lands short allowing opponent more time to react.

Ball lands deep allowing opponent less time to react

Fig. 6.4 Hitting deep allows opponent less time to hit the ball. These diagrams show two balls hit from the same place. In diagram A, the ball lands short, thus allowing the opponent more time to prepare for the shot. In B, the ball lands close to the opponent, thus allowing him less time for preparation. (A ball travels faster before bouncing than after hitting the ground.)

Playing the "low game." Advanced players who have mastered the slice off both wings can play a very effective game by hitting with good pace low over the net. Since a ball rises after being sliced, you do not have the problem of erring into the net. Balls that are sliced hard tend to stay low after they bounce, and by hitting short, you force your opponent to hit up and over the net. This produces errors.

If the slicer can hit low and to the *sides* of the court, the low game can be especially effective (*Fig. 6.5*). Occasionally, you can use this ball as an approach shot. Your opponent will be forced to hit up, and since he is off on one side of the court and near the net, an opening for your volley is created.

Fig. 6.5 Targets for advanced player's "low (slice) game."

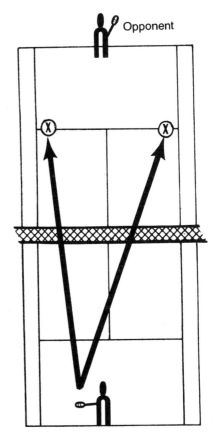

Opponent

Although your opponent is relatively close to the net, do not fear his coming all the way to the net from a sideline position. Net rushers are ineffective when approaching the net from such an angle; they prefer to come to the net from a center position. Naturally, it is difficult for the opponent to hit a powerful approach shot off a low ball.

Hitting the ball near the lines. It does not take a genius to realize that the closer you aim the ball to the boundary lines of the opponent's court, the greater the possibility of your making an error. Top players aim closer to lines than beginners. Rather than hitting safely down the middle, they have sufficient ball control to minimize errors while going close to lines. There is one very important question you must answer: "How close to the sidelines and baseline can I safely direct my shots?"

An excellent method of learning to place balls close to lines is to drill. For example, two players can benefit immeasureably by drilling forehands crosscourt. Both players should aim only a yard or two inside the lines since, in this noncompetitive situation, they have nothing to lose. Then, when they play a match, and allow themselves a safety margin of six to eight feet, they gain a feeling of confidence that they can hit accurately and safely.

The following example illustrates this. Paul, a "pusher" (one who does not take chances and swings slowly), is playing Charlie, who hits closer to lines and a little harder. Neither player has an adequate volley or a strong putaway shot from the back of the court. Paul can retrieve practically all of Charlie's shots. Since Charlie is taking the greater risk, he must realize that the longer a rally lasts, the poorer his chances are of winning the point. When you take a greater risk than your opponent by hitting closer to the lines, you must take measures to finish the point off, and not to prolong rallies.

If Paul's stamina is good, and he can continue to run down Charlie's more offensive shots, he will surely win the match (*Fig. 6.6*). Do not find yourself in Charlie's position of going near lines and hitting hard without having an adequate volley and overhead to finish the point.

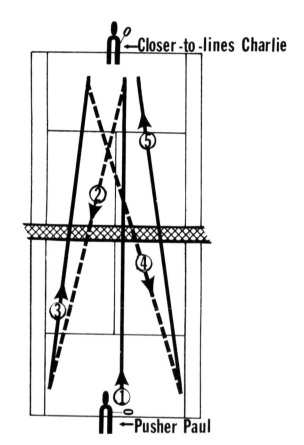

Fig. 6.6 If Paul can retrieve Charlie's risky shots, he will win the match by making fewer errors.

WHERE SHALL YOU AIM YOUR SHOTS?

Your target depends on your level of skill. As your ball control improves, your mental targets become smaller as you aim closer to lines. When using the targets in the accompanying illustrations, aim your ball toward the middle of each of the target areas listed by number (*Fig. 6.7*).

Fig. 6.7 Targets for various skill levels. Aim for the numbered areas.

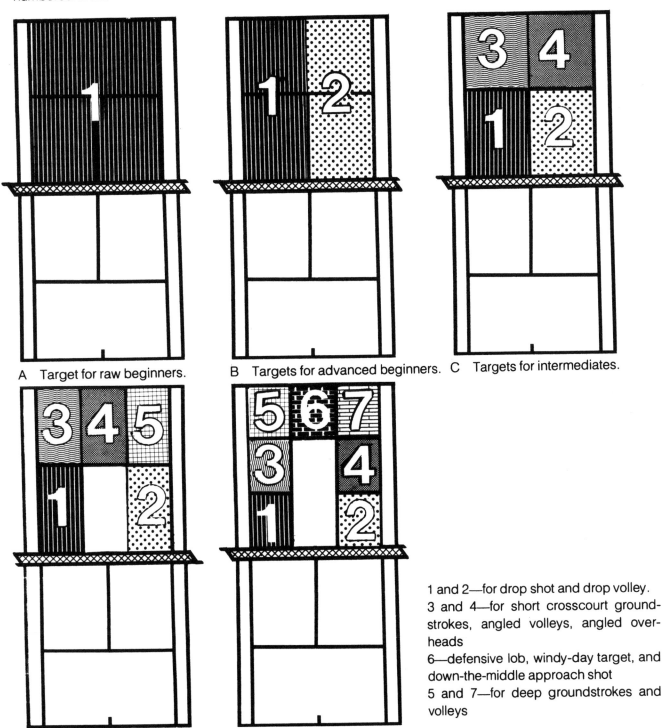

A   Target for raw beginners. B   Targets for advanced beginners. C   Targets for intermediates.

D   Targets for advanced players. E   Targets for tournament players.

1 and 2—for drop shot and drop volley.
3 and 4—for short crosscourt groundstrokes, angled volleys, angled overheads
6—defensive lob, windy-day target, and down-the-middle approach shot
5 and 7—for deep groundstrokes and volleys

27

Aiming toward the open court. After you develop ball-placement skills, the matter of where to direct your shots becomes somewhat simple. Aim most of your shots toward the opponent's weakness, or to the part of the court your opponent is farthest from. (As former baseball great Willie Keeler said, "Hit 'em where they ain't.") When you direct your shots to the area away from your opponent, you have two advantages: one, you have the best opportunity for an outright winning placement, a ball he is not able to touch; and two, you force him to hit while on the run rather than while set.

Aiming toward the corner of the court from which your opponent hit his last shot. Hitting two consecutive shots to the same corner, thereby getting your opponent off balance as he attempts to move back to the center of the court, is termed "hitting behind," or "wrong-footing," the player. This strategy is effective on any surface, but especially so on slippery clay, where changing direction is difficult.

Hitting crosscourt versus aiming down the line. When we speak of hitting down the line we mean hitting parallel with the sidelines (*Fig. 6.8*). Hitting crosscourt means hitting on a diagonal; this can be a shot of considerable distance (long crosscourt) or one of a shorter distance (short crosscourt) (*Fig. 6.9*).

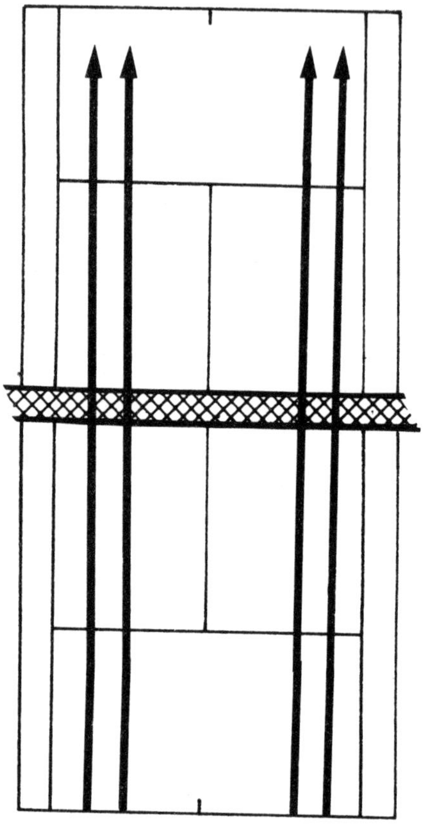

Fig. 6.8 Down-the-line shots travel parallel with the sidelines.

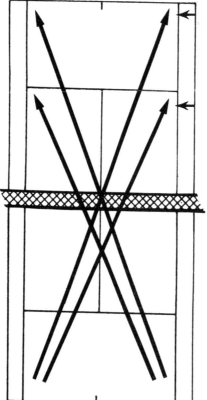

Fig. 6.9A Long crosscourt is used to move opponent without taking unnecessary risk.

B Short crosscourt is used for passing, and for running opponent great distances.

Fig. 6.9 Crosscourt shots travel in a diagonal direction.

Since the long crosscourt shot gives the stroker more space to direct the ball (a little more than six feet) than the down-the-line shot, there is greater safety in the long crosscourt play. Some players will restrict their blasting to the crosscourt direction. Another factor that makes the crosscourt a safer shot is that the net is three or four inches lower at the center, where the ball passes over, than it is near the singles sideline. In major tournaments, singles sticks are used to raise the sideline part of the net one or two inches higher than it is on an ordinary court. In this case the difference between the net height at the center and at the sidelines becomes even greater. The low ball that lands near the net is especially risky to hit over the high part of the net.

An important advantage of aiming your groundstrokes crosscourt is that you can run your opponent farther out of position than you can by using the down-the-line play. A very good crosscourt shot will move your opponent off court beyond the singles sideline (*Fig. 6.10*). However, angling an opponent off the court can occasionally backfire on the hitter, since angles created by our own shots leave openings for more severe angles from our opponent. Also, the sharper we make our crosscourt-angled shot, the less distance we have to keep the ball within the boundary line. Naturally, a very short crosscourt shot must be hit slowly and low over the net or it will land beyond the sideline.

Because of the three aforementioned advantages of stroking balls crosscourt (longer court, lower net, and running your opponent off court), some top players build their ground games on crosscourt shots. These same players rarely break a crosscourt rally by going down the line. By continuing a crosscourt rally they understand that when the angle of incidence (of the ball coming to them) equals the angle of reflection (the direction the ball returns to their opponent), there is less risk in the shot. It is easier and safer to return a ball in the same direction it came from.

Why all groundstrokes are not hit crosscourt. Given the preceding discussion, the reader will perhaps ask himself, Why not hit all groundstrokes crosscourt? There are four reasons why we do not follow this pattern:

1. Shot direction becomes very predictable. The opponent will always know where you are going to direct the ball and thus will have the advantage of waiting for the ball long before it arrives.

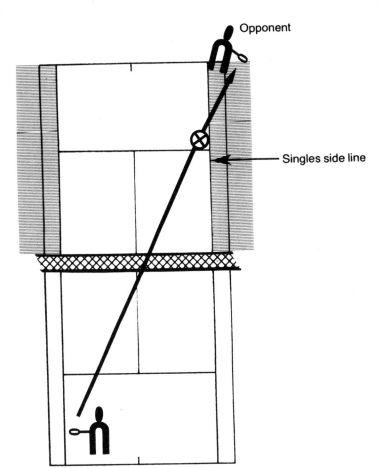

Fig. 6.10 A fine crosscourt shot moves opponent off court, past the singles sideline.

2. You cannot use the crosscourt ball as an approach shot, because it is difficult to attain good net position. As Jack Kramer stressed, a forehand crosscourt approach shot is usually a very low percentage play.

3. When you hit only crosscourt groundstrokes, you do not take advantage of a stroking weakness of an opponent. For example, if your right-handed opponent has a great forehand and a horrendous backhand, there is a possibility he should not be allowed to touch *any* forehands. Therefore, against him, you might never use a crosscourt forehand.

4. Your crosscourt shots might not come as naturally as your down-the-line shots. You might make more errors when you stroke crosscourt. There are many players who fall into this category, and there is a rather simple explanation for this rela-

tive lack of crosscourt-stroking skill. Practically all wall or backboard hitting is in the down-the-line direction. Also, warming up and simple rallying are done in a down-the-line direction. You should know in which direction you can hit your groundstrokes most effectively.

An additional comment should be made on the down-the-line slice. Usually, you should not attempt this shot on a low ball unless you are within about ten feet of the center mark, in order to minimize the danger of hitting the net at its highest point. By stroking in this inside-to-outside direction, you also take advantage of the natural outward spin of the slice (*Fig. 6.11*).

Fig. 6.11 Groundstroke-slicing down the line. Try to be no farther than ten feet from the center mark when slicing a low ball down the line. Down-the-line slices are effective because the spin breaks toward the outside of the court.

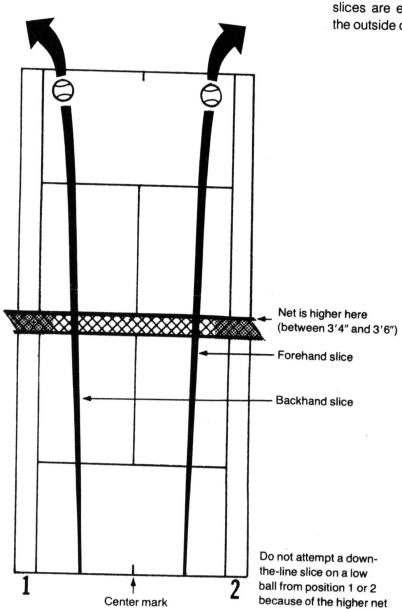

Net is higher here (between 3'4" and 3'6")

Forehand slice

Backhand slice

1

Center mark

2

Do not attempt a down-the-line slice on a low ball from position 1 or 2 because of the higher net

Try to utilize the crosscourt shot as much as possible, unless by doing so you are hitting into your opponent's strength, or you are more prone to errors when stroking crosscourt.

Should you aim to your opponent's backhand, or his forehand? Usually your opponent has one wing that is slightly weaker than the other. The difference between the two might be subtle but consequential. For example, if he hits nine out of ten good balls in the court with his forehand, and only seven out of ten with the backhand, this discrepancy can be capitalized on.

Be very alert to a change in the strength of an opponent's strokes, not only from match to match but from one set to another. An opponent can hit fine backhands during one set, and then suddenly the stroke can go off.

Characteristics of forehand and backhand. The muscles used on the forehand side are stronger than those on the backhand side, though there have been some exceptionally hard backhand hitters among world-class stars such as Don Budge. Therefore, forehand shots are usually more powerful than backhands. A hard overspin forehand is difficult for the net player to handle, and for this reason alone, many players prefer to attack and come to the net behind a ball hit to their opponent's backhand. On a forehand groundstroke, power can be generated quickly, and the direction of the passing shot can be disguised much more easily.

In addition to having power and overspin potential, the forehand is more flexible than the backhand. When forced to hit a groundstroke while moving away from the net, quite a number of players can hit a solid forehand. Rod Laver is one of the very few with this flexibility on the backhand wing.

Great forehands are usually hit with an Eastern or a semi-Western grip (*Fig. 6.12*). The Continental grip, in which the arm and wrist are not behind the racket as it strikes the ball, can produce a weak and erratic shot (*Fig. 6.13*). One of the most effective methods of breaking down a Continental forehand is to give your opponent high and soft balls to that side. Although the Continental or Australian grips have this weakness, they are extremely desirable for some strong-wristed players who want the simplicity of using one grip for all shots.

Compared with the forehand, the backhand groundstroke is usually slower and more difficult for most players to learn. However, once the shot is mastered, it often develops into a player's steadiest stroke. It is a natural shot, since the hitting arm is on the front shoul-

Fig. 6.12 **The Eastern-forehand grip has the most potential for power and control.**

Fig. 6.13 **The Continental grip can be very weak on high balls.**

der and is in a free position, not having to be brought across the body, as the forehand must.

In the beginning and intermediate levels of tennis it is usually advisable to play an opponent's backhand regularly. On the tournament level it often is best to hit to his forehand when both of you are in the backcourt. Of course, assume that you are able to run down his possibly powerful forehand shot. A major weakness in some forehands is that a number of players cannot temporize or slow down their swing, and thus can generate a fast string of errors. However, there are times when it will pay to stay away from the opponent's forehand unless you can hit in that direction with a lot of pace.

RUNNING AROUND, OR AVOIDING THE BACKHAND TO HIT THE FOREHAND

Desirablity of using this tactic. Some players will avoid using the backhand groundstroke whenever possible, preferring to take a few extra steps to put their forehand in play. This tactic can protect a stroking weakness, and can be extremely effective against a slow-ball hitter. To employ this tactic successfully you must be reasonably fast and in good condition. To minimize exhaustion, you should assume a home-base position slightly to the backhand side of the center mark.

When you avoid a backhand in this manner, the forehand becomes even more dangerous. Since the body automatically coils and the shoulders are forced to turn, you can hit with considerable power and accuracy.

Many top players run around a ball to take it with their strongest shot. Ken Rosewall, who has perhaps the greatest backhand in the world, nevertheless, will often step around a backhand and unleash his forehand to return a second serve. This is an excellent play. Bjorn Borg has played entire matches practically avoiding the backhand. Borg will often go so far as to stand in the doubles alley on the backhand side to hit a forehand during a rally! Frank Froehling III was taught by his father to avoid backhands at almost any cost. By doing this he developed one of the biggest forehands in the world.

Disadvantages of avoiding the backhand. On fast courts against hard hitters this is a difficult tactic to use consistently, since there is insufficient time to step around the ball. Therefore, those who do run around

their backhands will often find themselves using one technique on slow courts and a different style on faster surfaces. This is undesirable.

There are two additional disadvantages to running around the backhand: one, it is a tiring procedure that requires extra footwork; two, by stepping way over to the backhand side you often put yourself out of position for the next shot. This, of course, does not pertain when receiving service in the deuce court, as you run around a second serve heading toward your backhand side and take it with the forehand. In this instance, you are in a *better* position to receive the opponent's next shot than you would have been if you did not step around the backhand. Running around backhands when volleying is almost impossible because of the speed of the ball.

Tactics to use against a player who runs around his backhand. This can be a difficult person to play, because unless you can produce an answer to his

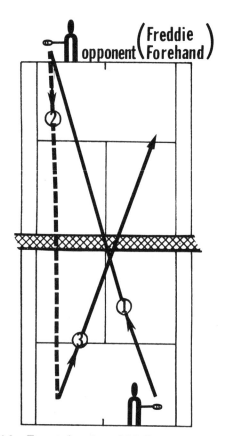

Fig. 6.14 Force forehand-hitting opponent to use backhand by aiming first ball to his forehand (1), and your second ball short (and angled) to his backhand side (3).

threat, you can easily find yourself under constant pressure from his big forehand. The most effective method of placing the ball on his backhand is first to direct it wide to his forehand and then to aim to his backhand. If you are still unable to force him to hit a backhand groundstroke, then simply direct all of your shots short, and preferably angled, to his backhand side (*Fig. 6.14*). The short backhand is difficult for him to run around.

When you are successful at forcing this type of player to use his backhand, be ready to advance to the net. Since he hits infrequently from that side, he is probably extremely weak there. Borg's two-handed backhand is unusual in that it remains formidable even though it is not used with the frequency of his forehand.

If you find it impossible to force your opponent to hit backhands, direct balls to his *forehand* side, where he does not have the opportunity to coil his body in a powerful position. However, guide some balls over to his backhand side in order to make him work to some extent.

HITTING AND PLAYING AGAINST HARD BALLS AND SOFT BALLS

Although a top tournament player hits hard, he can usually stroke softly as well, and knows how to play effectively against both types of hitters. International-class players, like all of us, were not able to hit with pace as beginners; they too started out as relatively unskilled and slow-stroking novices.

Beginner's push game. For the beginning player, pushing (swinging slow and hitting soft) is a relatively easy procedure. You simply loft the ball high over the net and drop it in the middle of the opponent's court. If you keep the ball six to, say, twelve feet above the net, and at least ten feet away from the nearest boundary line, making an error is almost an impossibility (*Fig. 6.15*). The beginning pusher takes the ball a little late (hitting the ball after the peak of its bounce) to afford himself plenty of time to stroke, as well as to allow his opponent's spins to dissipate. (A spin is most vicious immediately after the bounce, and it loses effectiveness after the ball reaches its peak.)

The advantage of the beginner's slow, high, down-the-middle pushing game is that it will help a player win matches at an early stage of development. To emerge victorious, the pusher relies on his opponent's errors, not his own winning shots. To employ this tactic

Fig. 6.15 Target for beginner's push game. Aim the ball high over the net.

he must run three or four times the distance of his opponent, so if running, stamina, and athletic ability are not his attributes, he should avoid engaging in this type of game. I used to play the beginner's push game and found that by doing this, I could almost, from the time I picked up a racket, beat fellows who had played the game for several years.

The disadvantages of playing the beginner's push game are many. First, you will be run to the brink of exhaustion, while your opponent is given a physical "reprieve." Second, there is no future in it, except for learning the lob, since you are hitting a ball with an abnormally high trajectory. If you are to become a reasonably strong player, you must learn to hit balls lower over the net and closer to the lines. Eventually, you should stroke the ball at its peak rather than take it late and low, as a beginning pusher might.

How to play against a beginner's push game.
Breaking down a player who hits every ball high and
down the center is an easy task for an intermediate
who has a putaway groundstroke, or a volley and a
smash. The latter two shots are the most effective
weapons in exploiting the beginner's push game.
However, most fledglings do not have these strokes.

If you do not have an adequate net game, the next-
best tactic is to hit short and bring the pusher to the
net, where he will be forced to volley or smash. Some
pushers, after being brought into the midcourt area on
a short ball, will return quickly to the baseline rather
than volley or smash. In this case an even shorter ball
has to be hit to make sure that the pusher cannot retreat to his secure refuge in the back of his court.

If you cannot make headway against the beginning,
down-the-middle-style pusher by attacking him and
coming to the net, or by hitting short and bringing him
to the net, then perhaps you should try to outpush him
as a last resort. Hit high and down the middle of the
court and see if he loses patience and starts to attack
with low-percentage shots.

Advanced push game. Unlike the simple push
game of the beginner, which is ineffective against a
good tennis player, a tournament push game with slow
conditions (slow court and slow balls) can be extremely difficult to cope with. (A slow hitter's best opportunities are on the local or sectional level; his type of game
is becoming increasingly rare on the international
scene.) An advanced pusher, who usually functions
best in European tournaments, is one who prefers to
hit with little pace from the baseline. Although most
advanced pushers are not inclined to come to the net,
some utilize a sound forecourt game with their slow-
ball tactics. In some of his notable clay-court victories,
Herb Flam combined a deadly volley with a groundstroke pushed ten feet above the net. For five years
Flam was ranked in the top ten in the world.

The international-class pusher will never advance
past the first or second round at Wimbledon, the Australian Nationals, or any other fast-court tournament.
Nor is he capable of winning the important slow-court
tournaments of the world such as the French or Italian
championships. At Paris or Rome he will frequently
have the good win, but since his play requires bound-
less physical and mental energy, he has difficulty
stringing a series of individual victories together. Although world-class pushers can stroke passing shots
extremely well, they lack the all-court game and ball
speed necessary to become multisurface champions.

Although a big hitter can have some dreadful days
on a tennis court, not so with a high-class pusher. He
rarely has a bad loss on slow clay. A hard hitter often
loses numerous games to someone below his level in
ability, whereas the steady player makes his opponent
earn everything he receives. The tournament pusher is
often feared since he does not give away cheap
points. Because of his tenacity and court intelligence,
the international-class pusher is a breed to be ad-
mired.

There are players besides Herb Flam whom I would
place in the international-class-pusher category. William Alvarez, of Colombia, Eduardo Zuleta, of Ecua-
dor, and Warren Woodcock, of Australia, were in this
classification. Woodcock had a marshmallow of a
serve but gained numerous scalps on clay. When Ian
Tiriac, of Rumania, was father-confessor and patient
tennis pro of a young Ilie Nastase, he was a fine international-class pusher.

The advanced push game is suited for you if you
have limited serving potential, have only minimal power off forehand or backhand, hit groundstrokes early,
possess excellent speed afoot, have a fine sense of
balance, have good stamina, and are in your late
teens, twenties, or early thirties. Forget this game if
you intend to spend most of your future playing days
on hard courts. It is best to employ this tactic on
brown-clay courts. Advanced pushing can be moder-
ably effective on the green-clay-like courts of the eastern and southern U.S. However, since the green clay
affords the attacker some speed, the pusher must be
very careful with his shots, or he can be blasted off the
court.

In order to play the advanced push game well, you
should hit almost all of your groundstrokes with overspin. The main reason for this is that in order to attain
the uncanny steadiness necessary to this type of
game, you cannot divide your time hitting slices,
chops, flat balls, and so on. The second reason that
overspin is necessary is that the advanced pusher-
retriever is attacked constantly, so his topspin passing
shots must be precise. When a player uses overspin
on all his groundstrokes, he is, in actuality, working on
his passing shots all of the time. Therefore, when his
opponent ventures to the net, the overspin pusher has
his tough passing shots ready in razor-sharp condition. Guillermo Vilas, of Argentia, though not a pusher,
has an excellent defense against a net rusher because he hits almost all overspins.

The advanced pusher often has set targets. Tony

Vincent, an American, utilized this strategy during the many years he competed in Europe. Starting the point off with a slow serve (hardly ever hitting a fault, much less a double fault), he would place practically all of his baseline shots (not passing shots) in one of two places. One target was located in the middle of his opponent's backhand side of the backcourt area, and the second was at the same place on the forehand side (*Fig. 6.16*). His groundstrokes would pass three to four feet above the net as he guided them toward each target. Because he used only two basic targets against almost everyone he played, he was like a machine in executing this play. He almost never missed.

The majority of Vincent's opponents preferred to attack him. Lew Hoad, who was then one of the greatest players in the world, fell before Vincent's slow- and medium-paced balls at Monte Carlo. During his prime, Vincent would not come out of his backcourt shell to attack, and when his opponent chose also to dig in behind his baseline, the rallies became endless. Naturally, there was excruciating predictability in Vincent's game. He, like certain other pushers, was a tough customer in his heyday; it was highly improbable that anyone who tangled with him in a baseline battle on a slow court would not be beaten, physically and in the score.

There have been numerous cases in which a fine player would almost give away a match rather than become involved in a brutally punishing contest with a pusher. Although Harold Solomon hits with good pace, he remains on the baseline on slow courts, and is occasionally awarded such a "semidefault" victory.

Nicolò Pietrangeli, an Italian clay backcourt artist, threw in the towel a time or two against William Alvarez. Pietrangeli was ranked seven times in the world's top ten. As the years wore on, in their encounters, he found Alvarez's game more and more wearing and unpalatable. As spectacular as Pietrangeli's shots were (brilliant slices, sharply angled overspin drives off both sides, delicate drop shots), he could not beat his "human backboard" opponent without suffering through a grueling match. As a result, he occasionally took the easy way out.

How to play against an advanced push game. First of all, you have to be in good physical condition to play a steady player, because you are going to be out on the court a long time. Furthermore, you will probably find it additionally fatiguing to generate your own pace. You must map out a careful battle plan and adhere to it rigidly. Retrievers and pushers thrive on the doubt and indecision of their opponents. A pusher's foe is in deep trouble when, in the middle of a match, he starts having such thoughts as, "I don't know whether or not I should attack his second serve," or, "I don't know whether I should serve and volley." You must be resolute in executing your plan.

One of the easiest methods of defeating a tournament-level pusher is to attack him on almost every ball, providing you have a *great* net game. One year an Australian touring player, Mervyn Rose, who had a reputation as a fine forecourt player, came to Miami Beach to play in the Good Neighbor tournament. I watched him work out before the tournament and noticed he was a left-hander and was slightly over-

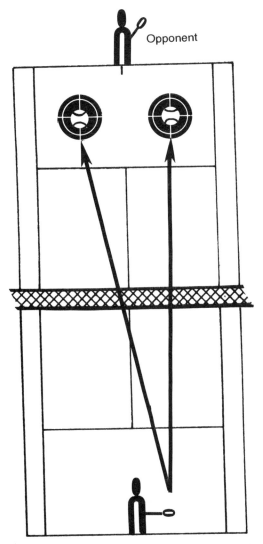

Fig. 6.16 Targets for advanced pusher when opponent is at baseline.

weight. In addition, he was a rarity in tennis in that he frequently smoked cigarettes. Rose was scheduled to play Tony Vincent in an early round, and my curiosity was sufficiently aroused to bring me out to the courts to observe. Would Rose be able to employ his net game against Vincent, or would he be caught in a bitter baseline struggle? They completed their warmup shots and started play. Rose served and volleyed out the first game on the green-clay surface. When Vincent served the second game and stayed in the back of his court, Rose quickly came in and played that game from the net as well. His overhead and volley were incredible as he won game after game by hitting a minimum number of groundstrokes. Rose finished off his steady opponent in less than an hour, allowing him only a couple of games. He was breathing quite easily as he shook hands with Vincent, lighted a cigarette, and headed to the locker room. After watching Rose perform that day, it was no surprise to learn that he eventually was ranked in the world's top ten. He possessed the perfect tools to carve up an advanced pusher. Rose's one-sided annihilation of Vincent was a dramatic example of the inherent weakness of pushing in international-class tennis.

Since pushers usually use their opponent's pace to give themselves ball speed, they can be in trouble if they are denied this pace. A number of years ago a French Davis Cup player, Jean-Noël Grinda, effectively used this tactic of making the pusher generate his own pace. Grinda was an unusually handsome fellow, about six feet seven inches tall, and extremely strong and well proportioned. He was a playboy with plenty of money who dated some of the most attractive women in the world.

Grinda managed to break away long enough from one of his dates in St. Petersburg, Florida, to play world-class pusher, Eduardo Zuleta, in the Master's tournament there. On the morning of the match I met Jean at the club, and we went through his prematch routine together. We jogged, did a few limbering-up exercises, and hit some balls. Grinda then went to play Zuleta. I decided to watch, and proceeded to take a seat in the bleachers. Along came Eddie Moylan, who sat beside me. Moylan was a world-class player, and later the Cornell University tennis coach. As Grinda was cracking his huge serve in the warmup, and Zuleta was returning every ball, I asked Moylan who he thought would win the match. He replied, "Grinda, love and love." I answered, "How can anyone come close to beating Zuleta badly on clay? He has just

beaten Roy Emerson and Mike Davies, and spends an hour and a half a day on the backboard alone. He makes *no* unforced errors in a match." Moylan said, "Watch!"

The match began with Grinda's bludgeoning a serve and the Ecuadorian's returning it effortlessly with his sliced forehand. (Zuleta was the most successful player ever to use the undercut-forehand groundstroke exclusively.) Grinda then hit a lob down the middle of the court, which Zuleta returned, and Grinda did it again and again until he extracted a ball that was a little short. Grinda then hit a deep approach shot and took the net position. Zuleta threw up a high lob and the Frenchman smashed the ball away. Grinda denied pace to his small-but-talented opponent. He won not only the first game but the next eleven in a row, for the match. Grinda beat this fine pusher 6–0, 6–0. Moylan's prophesy was incredible. He realized that Grinda was a master of the art of denying pace to a pusher, and that he had the weapons to finish off a point as well.

Thus, the "pushing" game is an extremely effective one to use up to a certain level of play. With very slow courts and balls, or against opponents who lack mental toughness, pushers can occasionally get an international-class scalp. However, in this day and age, pushers are effective only on a lower tournament level. The greatest players do not push, they hit hard, and hitting hard is what we will discuss next.

How to hit hard with effectiveness. Why is hitting a hard ball advantageous? To put it briefly and simply, when a player is on the receiving end of a fast ball, the timing becomes difficult and errors occur more frequently than with balls that are hit slowly. Also, the power hitter does not have to move as much. It is very difficult to jockey a hard hitter around with touch and drop shots. In addition, the hard hitter has more possibilities of placing balls out of his opponent's reach. The soft-ball hitter must rely on the opponent's error; he usually cannot make the winning placement.

A hard ball is the result of a long and fast swing of the tennis racket. Swinging quickly requires better timing than swinging slowly. A player who swings hard successfully must have hit a great number of balls in his lifetime, and must play very regularly to retain his sharpness and his sound form A slow-ball hitter who uses a high trajectory over the net can, in an unorthodox manner, shovel a ball over the net and keep it in play. Not so with a hard hitter.

Players who are slow afoot *must* hit hard to be effective. The catlike player has an option of how he wants to style his game. Size and strength are usually assets for blasting, although there are some bantam-weights who can cream the ball as well. There was a tremendous 135-pound Italian player, Fausto Gardini, who used to crunch his forehand. "The spider" would almost dive into the ball to get his pace on the forehand drive.

Hitting hard should be a natural result of proper stroking, good timing, a loose backswing, and keeping the racket strings on the ball as long as possible after contact. The player who wishes to stroke with brisk pace should grip the racket as far down the handle as possible, to obtain maximum leverage. Since over-hitting is common among players learning to hit hard, it is important to make sure your out balls do not go more than three or four feet beyond the opponent's baseline or sideline. Also, you know you are swinging too hard when your balls miss badly by going into the bottom of the net rather than striking the tape at the top of the barrier.

Stroking with good pace has to be a normal part of a player's game; it is not to be turned on one day and off the next. Ordinarily, you should use the same speed of swing, regardless of whether you hit on a backboard, drill on a court, play practice sets, or are battling in the final of the U.S. Open.

The intelligent player must understand that there will be a few instances when he will lack rhythm, and he should not continue to sock the ball until he has regained it. He must be aware of the type of shots that cause him to make errors (low-percentage shots). The experienced player knows, for example, that hardly anyone except a Jimmy Connors can slug a very low ball as it is coming up from the ground and keep it in the court. Hard hitters quickly realize that the long crosscourt groundstroke has the best chance of remaining in the court (*Fig. 6.17*). Moderate overspin is a necessary companion for successful hard-hit groundstrokes. Ellsworth Vines, an extremely hard hitting player, probably had good reason for a switch to golf at the height of his career. Because he lacked overspin, his margin of error was very small, and, as a result, he was prone to bad and frustrating losses.

A sound volley must be brought along with any hard-hitting game, since without one, you will not win enough points to make the inherent risks worthwhile. Power hitting with big approach shots makes volleying that much easier, since the opponent has difficulty making precise and low passing shots.

As he hits the ball from corner to corner, the hard hit-

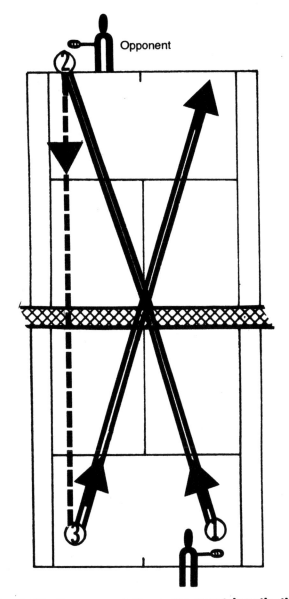

Fig. 6.17 Because of the extra court length, the long crosscourt shots (1 and 3) are desirable for the hard hitter who wants to minimize errors.

ter is hoping to elicit an error; however, he is primarily looking to extract a short ball. How well a tournament-tennis player takes advantage of the short ball seems to determine his level of play as much as anything else. The shot that international-class players excel at is the short ball putaway (*see Fig. 6.1, page 21*). By "putaway" I mean just that: no second chances for the opponent who gives you a short and soft ball. Most top players use their forehand for the putaway; a player is indeed fortunate if he has a backhand-groundstroke putaway as well.

How to play against a hard hitter. When you compete against a hard-hitting tennis player, you must know at the outset that you will have to run faster and farther than he. In addition, you will feel some pressure in attempting to return his bombs. The hard hitter, however, will have the added strain of knowing that *he* has to produce the winner or force the error to gain a point. Good footing is necessary against a hard hitter; you can forget about beating a slugger who is at your level of ability if you are pitted against him on slippery clay. A court that produces bad bounces also favors the hard hitter. When a slowly hit ball takes a bad bounce, the receiver often has time to react, but when a hard-hit ball takes a bad bounce, there is little the player can do.

To be able to cope with hard hitters in matches, you must meet them in practice (just as you must meet other types, including pushers and left-handers). Naturally, you should try to minimize your errors and lengthen points. Usually, the longer the rally is extended, the poorer are the hitter's chances of winning the point.

Hard hitters thrive on confidence. If they acquire a comfortable lead, they often relax, loosen up, and play better. When this happens, it can become, for the opponent, a "Katie bar the door" situation: the hitter is then impossible to stop as he gains momentum. Conversely, if hitters become tense or uncertain, there is no other type of player who can give you unearned points more quickly. You are in trouble when competing against the player who hits with good pace *and* controls the ball because of built-in safety factors in his game (some overspin and underspin on groundstrokes, and overspin on service).

Ordinariliy, stay away from the net position when you play the slugger, since he hits what amounts to a passing shot on nearly every ball. In other words, he is firmly grooved on his passing shots long before you decide to come to the net.

Try to stroke balls deep to him so you will have more time to retrieve his hard shots. You can also slice low over the net to force him to hit up. Hitting high loops can force him to come to the net to attack you. If his volley is suspect, this tactic can be effective.

TAKING GROUNDSTROKES EARLY

You can gain backcourt offense and move your opponent with another method besides hitting hard groundstrokes. This tactic is to stand closer to the net than you ordinarily would and take most of your groundstrokes no more than two feet behind the baseline, and preferably *inside* it. By doing this, you can control points against players who might have moved you like a monkey on a string had you taken the normal position farther behind the baseline. Eventually, you should try this technique while warming up or rallying. You might have to shorten your swing to be successful with it.

While groundstroking from a position on or inside the baseline, you are often hitting the ball on the rise, which is difficult for the player who is just beginning to learn the game. When beginners receive deep balls, they should retreat quickly behind the baseline and hit safe groundstrokes. The half volley or quick pickup should be avoided by novices.

An advocate of this style of play was the phenomenal Italian clay-court artist Guiseppe Merlo. He had a serve that was only about half the speed of most international-class players. He used a two-handed backhand, and choked up on the handle for his right-handed forehand. Neither his volley nor his overhead was outstanding. He strung his racket at about twenty pounds pressure; one could move the strings back and forth with no effort at all. There was almost no sound from the strings as they contacted the ball. Now you are probably wondering what this little chap had that enabled him to defeat the greatest players in the world on clay.

Merlo stood inside the baseline to hit most of his groundstrokes, and he hit with good pace. He directed his shots differently from other top players who place their shots from one corner of the baseline to the other. He angled short along the sidelines, sending his opponents far off court to retrieve each shot. By stroking balls from inside his baseline, Merlo seldom had to venture more than three yards or so from the center mark. No top player worked less than he In a match, and certainly no one controlled more points on clay courts. To be on the opposite side of the net from Merlo on a slow clay court was a brutal experience. He ran you great distances with his angled shots, and because he was hitting the ball early, you had to go on an all-out sprint to reach each ball. The first time I played him I could not believe a player could hit balls as close to the lines as he did and yet keep them in play for an entire match (*Fig. 6.18*).

The best defense to use against this type of player is to hit very deep balls, forcing him nearly to half-volley his groundstrokes. Another effective tactic is to hit high overspin loops. You can also try using the drop shot, to force him to play in the forecourt. Actually, a player's only *solid* defense against a skilled Merlo-type player is to play him on grass or other fast courts. Wimbledon used to invite him, out of respect for victories achieved on clay courts. But he was helpless on quick surfaces, since his serve and his forecourt game were weak. Harold Solomon is a current star who has been ineffective at Wimbledon for this reason.

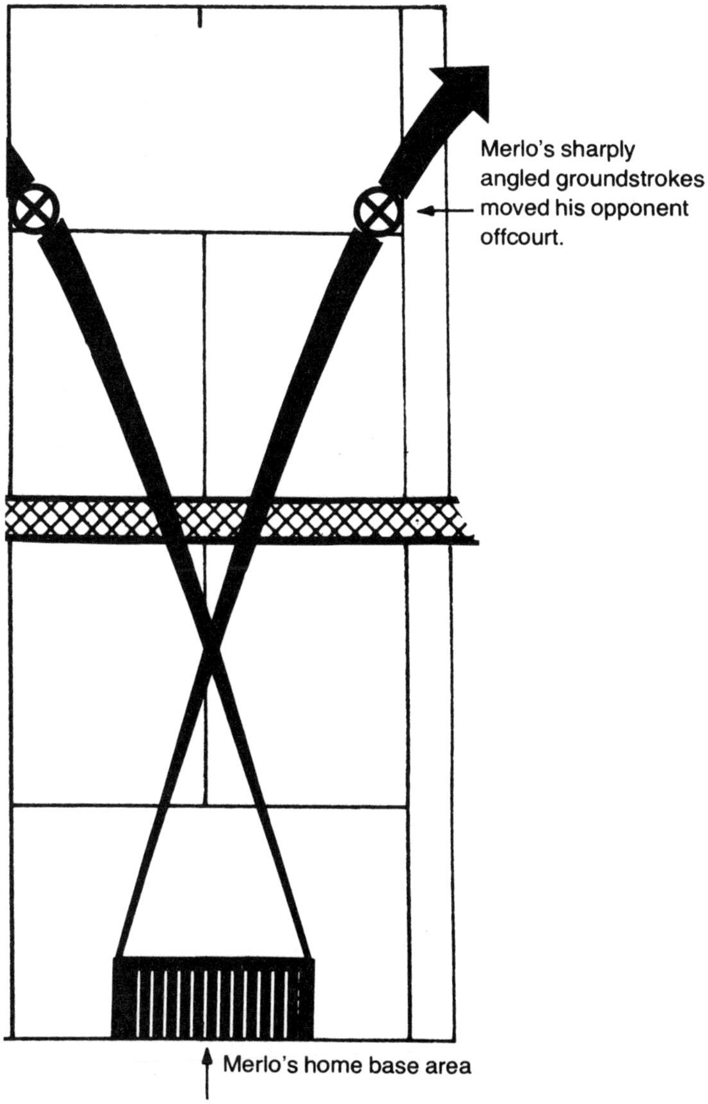

STAYING IN THE BACK OF THE COURT ON ALL SHOTS

If you have a game similar to Merlo's, which is rather ineffective at the net, think about playing a match and not coming to the forecourt unless you are forced into it. Just because famous tennis stars spend a considerable amount of time volleying and smashing, this does not mean you ought to. There are two main reasons for staying on the baseline: first, your lack of a forecourt game; and second, your opponent's superb passing shots.

The biggest disadvantage of not coming to the net is that a wise opponent will sense this and be content to hit safe mid-court balls against you; he does not have to risk deeper and more dangerous shots landing near your baseline. Also, your opponent is able to concentrate on the ball more, since he does not have to keep an eye on you to determine whether you are at the net or in the backcourt.

USING LONG AND SHORT TACTICS

An effective method of moving an opponent is to utilize the long-and-short tactical pattern of baseline play. You first hit a deep (long) ball into one of the opponent's corners. You then follow it with a short ball to the opposite side, forcing him to run as much as possible (*Fig. 6.19*).

USING LOOPS TO EXTRACT THE SHORT BALL

The loop is a groundstroke resembling an offensive lob and is used when both players are in the back of the court. It is especially effective when stroked with overspin against short players, since the ball will bounce very high and force them to take it at an awk-

Merlo's sharply angled groundstrokes moved his opponent offcourt.

Merlo's home base area

Fig. 6.18 Guiseppe Merlo's pattern of tennis play. He seldom retreated more than a foot or two behind the baseline, and took many balls on the rise.

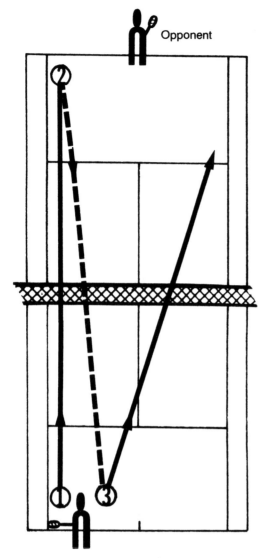

Opponent

Fig. 6.19 Long (1) and short (3) groundstroke combination.

wardly high position. (*Fig. 6.20*). When receiving the loop, a player's alternatives are to half-volley the ball, to take it at the difficult head-level height, or to retreat almost to the fence in order to take it at waist level. Since a loop does not offer any pace, it is difficult to hit a hard ball off it without an error. The loop is an especially good shot to use on clay against a person who has spent most of his playing days on cement, where one rarely sees this shot. When a player is on the receiving end of high loops, he often becomes exasperated and mentally fatigued from grappling with a ball that offers him no leverage or stroking power.

One of the most effective ways to cope with loops is to stand slightly inside your baseline and to move in and volley them. There are also times when you should half-volley loops, especially when playing against the wind. If you are getting the worst of exchanges when your opponent is hitting loops, you may be forced to start a net attack. Another possibility is to start drop-shotting the person who loops, since he is often a backcourt specialist with little inclination to come to the net. An additional method of deterring a loop attack is to hit loops back to the instigator, giving him a taste of his own medicine. Be sure to include in your practice schedule some players who loop so that you will be accustomed to this vexing shot in a match.

BLUFFING A TRIP TO THE NET

There is a baseline tactic that will occasionally mislead your opponent into attempting a dangerous passing shot when he should not be using one at all. This is the bluff, or fake, toward the net, when you and your opponent are in the back of the court. The bluff takes place immediately after you hit your shot, when you take one fast step toward the net and then quickly halt your advance.

Why is this particular bluff successful? If your opponent is a good player, he wants always to know where you are on the court. Although they usually know your whereabouts, most top players keep their eyes closely on the ball throughout the point. There is only one instance when your opponent brings both your body and the ball into his vision: this is just as you are stroking the ball. It is in this split second following your stroke that he is frequently susceptible to your fake. Although stamping feet on the ground is considered an unethical tactic, a legitimate body movement toward the net is well within the ethical framework of the game. After your one-step bluff is made, you must move very quickly back to your home base in order to be ready for the next shot (*Fig. 6.21*). Sometimes a bluff to the net can backfire when you recover too slowly and your opponent blasts a shot deep at your feet.

We have covered baseline play, which is the backbone of a good tennis game. Since some baseline players can keep the ball in play from the backcourt indefinitely, we must attack them by advancing to the net. Making a sound approach shot is essential before we can turn our volley and overhead loose in the battle, and this will be the subject of the next chapter.

A   Shot is made

Fig. 6.20 Loops can force opponent to stroke balls above their head.

Fig. 6.21 Bluffing an advance to the net off a backhand stroke.

B   Fake is made by stepping toward opponent with right foot

C   Recovery is made to home base

Chapter 7

APPROACH-SHOT TACTICS

The approach shot is an offensive groundstroke that the player follows from the backcourt to the net. The approach shot usually falls into one of two tactical patterns: first, you can come to the net behind a well-prepared and penetrating approach shot and win the point with an easy volley or smash. In making such a deep and precise approach shot (see Tilden's criteria later in this chapter) you are taking some risk even before advancing to the forecourt. The second tactic is to take less of a chance by stroking a shorter and softer approach shot and to be faced with a more difficult volley or smash. With this tactic, the ball is kept away from lines so that errors are rare.

Regardless of which of the two approach-shot tactics you use, develop an understanding of the kinds of approaches that will win you points. All of your approach shots should be carefully planned; you should never use the "coming in on a wing and a prayer" approach.

Although a player can advance to the net on any kind of ball, a true approach shot is an attacking play, and usually comes about as a result of a weak shot by the opponent.

By advancing from the backcourt to the forecourt, you place pressure on your opponent. Your movement to the net often causes him to take his eyes off the ball and make errors. When you are at the net and he is behind his baseline, his targets are reduced, and he often feels *he* must do something extraordinary, such as making a clean passing shot or an untouchable lob.

To make your advance to the net more effective, try periodically to use the fake, or bluff, approach discussed in the previous chapter. By employing the occasional bluff, you will often be given an easy volley when you do come to the net, since your opponent can mistakenly think you are still in the backcourt. Once in a while, you can sneak to the net by not starting forward immediately after hitting your approach shot. By delaying your start toward the net a second or two, it is possible to conceal your move.

WHEN SHOULD YOU HIT AN APPROACH SHOT?

First, it should be said that the acid test of the effect of your approach shots is the question "Are you winning the majority of points when you do it?" If your approach shot is hit softly and down the middle but you are scoring well from it, use it! Conversely, if you are making picture-book approach shots but losing points to your opponent's great passing shots, or to your own volleying errors, forget about that particular method; perhaps you should not come to the net at all. The value of an approach shot is its effectiveness against your opponent. Bear in mind that one type of approach shot might be successful against Player A but might not work against Player B.

What kind of ball should you follow to the net? In general, it is advisable to make an approach shot on a ball landing inside one of your service boxes. In addition, you should be standing inside your baseline while hitting the approach *(Fig. 7.1)*. The use of either of these guidelines will help guarantee that you will be reasonably close to the net as you hit your first volley. By moving close to the net, you minimize the opponent's ability to hit hard-to-return balls at your feet.

However, there are instances when you should not come to the net on a short ball. For example, if your opponent hit a short but low scorching drive that you almost had to dig out of the ground, you might have difficulty making a solid, hard, accurate shot. In addition, it would be risky trying to move toward the net as you hit such a dangerous ball.

Another tempting but low-percentage ball for you to answer with an approach shot is the one hit short to you but angled sharply. Do not advance to the net if you are coming in from near the doubles alley on the side of the court, because your body weight is moving in the wrong direction *(Fig. 7.2)*.

There are occasions when you should run to the net even after hitting a ball from behind your baseline. Let us say you have a great volley but a mediocre ground-

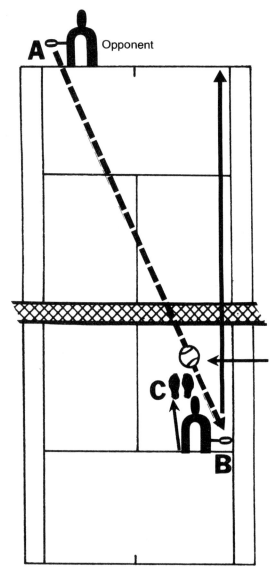

Fig. 7.1   Order of shots
A.   Opponent hits short ball (ball bounces here)
B.   Make an approach shot
C.   Advance to net

Fig. 7.1   Suggestions for hitting approach shot.
Make the approach shot and advance to the net when you are inside the court boundaries, and the opponent's moderate-speed ball has landed short.

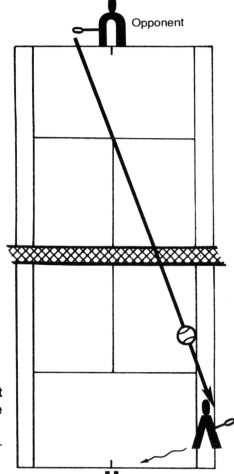

Fig. 7.2   When the opponent angles you off court with a groundstroke, do not try to advance to the net.
After returning your opponent's angled shot, return immediately to home base (H).

stroke game, and your opponent does not have good passing shots but is very steady. In this case, coming to the net might be a wise percentage play for you, especially on grass or other relatively fast surfaces. (Several nationally ranked Californians hit "approach shots" from as far behind the baseline as two yards.) Another instance that might warrant an approach to the net from behind the baseline is when your opponent is one who does not use the lob. In this situation it is advisable to use a *slow* loop, to allow you plenty of time to advance very close to the net.

Tilden's three approach-shot ingredients. Bill Tilden, the great American tennis player, competed in tournaments primarily during the 1920s and '30s. Since his standards for approach shots were as demanding as any known, we will use them as a takeoff point for discussion. Tilden said that approach shots should have the following three elements:

1. Your approach shot should force your opponent to move as he strokes his passing shot. (Naturally, if he is forced to move, he will not have the power and accuracy that he otherwise would have.)

2. An approach shot should be hit with excellent pace. (Tilden reasoned that it is much more difficult for the opponent to attain the accuracy to pass you if he is given a very hard ball to hit.)

3. An approach shot should be placed within a yard of the opponent's baseline. (This is to drive your opponent as far back in his court as possible, so that you will have ample time to cut off his attempted passing shot.)

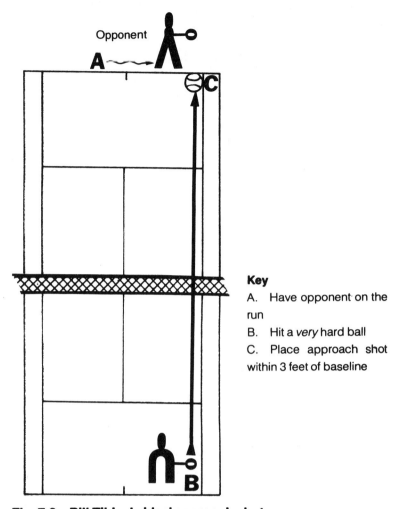

Key
A. Have opponent on the run
B. Hit a *very* hard ball
C. Place approach shot within 3 feet of baseline

Fig. 7.3   Bill Tilden's ideal approach shot.

What Tilden proposed was the ideal approach shot. If allowed to advance to the net position behind such a perfectly executed shot, the worst volleyer in the world would score at will. Tilden advocated coming to the net "loaded for bear" (*Fig. 7.3*).

Strict adherence to Tilden's three approach-shot principles would produce adverse results for most players. To begin with, we would be at the net much less often, and this would be disastrous for many fast-court players. Although Tilden had a fine analytical mind, he competed in an era when players believed that a good baseline or ground game was the answer to the net-rushing game. When competing on medium-speed or fast surfaces, most of today's players feel just the reverse. In modern high-level competition a player will often lose if he spends too much time trying to maneuver an opponent about the court so that

he will have him on the run when he approaches the net.

Tilden advised that we should hit our approach shots hard. This is a good way to extract an error, but control can be a problem. An added, and peculiar, difficulty is that the ball we hit hard will be returned that much faster. We will not be able to advance as close to the net as we would if we hit the ball not quite as hard. For this reason, some players prefer their opponents to attack with flat rather than sliced (slower) approach shots.

You recall Tilden's third premise—that approach shots should land within three feet of your opponent's baseline. This is a very dangerous practice. How many of even the world's greatest players can consistently place their approach shots this close to the baseline without making errors? Not many. Most are wise in allowing themselves a safety margin of a few extra feet.

Conclusions about spin versus flat, and hard versus soft, approach shots. A key factor in deciding whether you should hit approach shots with or without spin is the amount of control you possess in handling short balls. It is important to realize that when you are hitting groundstrokes from well within your baseline, there is much less distance for your hard balls to drop in your opponent's court than if you were hitting from ten or twelve feet behind the baseline. In other words, it is very easy to make errors on approach shots by hitting them long *(Fig. 7.4)*.

Control is a necessity on approach shots, and spin results in control. Placing overspin on the forehand approach shot is a wise tactic. A slice (underspin and sidespin) is often your best play on low forehands, and on practically all backhands. A low and short ball to the backhand almost must be undercut. A firmly sliced groundstroke, in addition to affording control, keeps the ball low, making the opponent's passing shot more difficult to execute. As was previously mentioned, the sliced approach shot allows the hitter more time to position himself at the net than the flat or overspin shot. The underspin approach shot is especially good if your opponent has presented you with a short ball, has good baseline position, and is not running one

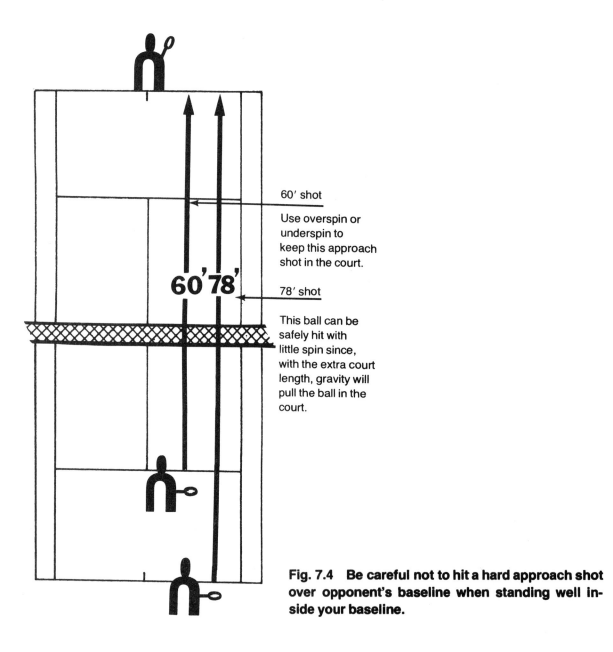

60' shot

Use overspin or underspin to keep this approach shot in the court.

60'78'

78' shot

This ball can be safely hit with little spin since, with the extra court length, gravity will pull the ball in the court.

Fig. 7.4 Be careful not to hit a hard approach shot over opponent's baseline when standing well inside your baseline.

way or the other. In other words, when your opponent is well ensconced in the backcourt, there is no compelling rush to get the ball to him. In this case, depth is more important than pace.

To take advantage of your opponent when he is out of position, you should hit a hard approach shot away from him, toward the open part of the court. An approach shot is doubly valuable if the ball is taken early, or at least not allowed to drop below waist height. After maneuvering him slightly off court, you should stroke the ball back to his side of the court as quickly as possible. This rushes the opponent and minimizes his chances of hitting a good passing shot or lob. Those readers who have encountered an attacking slugger who takes the ball early know how futile a defense is: to survive, you are almost totally dependent on his making errors.

Another excellent approach-shot tactic is to use slow-to-normal pace on your regular backcourt shots and then to increase the pace to fast-to-normal on your approach shots. This can upset an opponent's timing.

SHOULD APPROACH SHOTS BE HIT DOWN THE LINE OR CROSSCOURT?

Down-the-line approach shots enable us to advance closer to the net than those hit crosscourt. Since we should take net position slightly to the side of the center line that our opponent is hitting the ball from (*Fig. 7.5*), the down-the-line approach shot enables us to achieve proper forecourt position in a shorter period of time (*Fig. 7.6*).

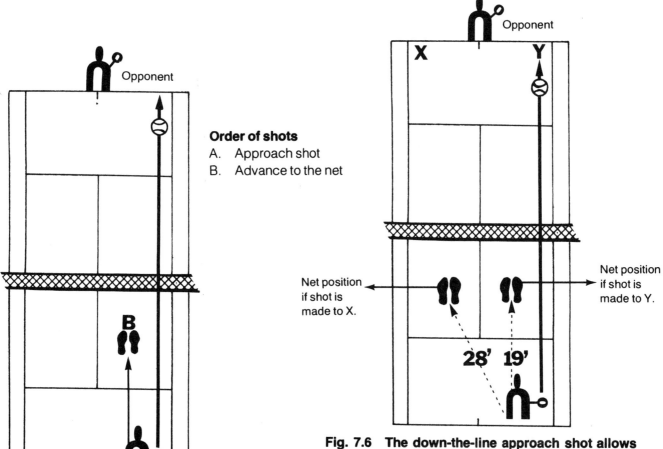

Order of shots
A. Approach shot
B. Advance to the net

Fig. 7.5 Take net position on the same side the opponent will hit the ball from.

Fig. 7.6 The down-the-line approach shot allows better forecourt position than the crosscourt approach shot. When the approach shot is made down the line to corner Y, you gain proper net position much quicker than hitting crosscourt to corner X.

When you are facing another right-hander, almost always aim your forehand approach shot down the line, to his backhand. Tactically, the forehand-crosscourt approach shot is tantamount to hara-kiri.

It is more difficult to decide in which direction you should hit the backhand approach shot. Should you go down the line, into his probable strength, or crosscourt, to his weakness? This is a difficult choice and can be made only after comparing your approach shots with the passing shots of your opponent.

Down-the-middle approach shots. If neither the down-the-line nor the crosscourt-backhand approach shot is paying dividends for you, contemplate hitting down the middle of the court to your opponent *(Fig. 7.7)*. The main advantage of the down-the-middle approach shot is that it reduces the hitting angle for your opponent's passing shots. It also eliminates the possibility of your erring wide of the sideline. The primary disadvantage of the down-the-middle approach is that it allows your opponent the choice of returning your ball with his strongest groundstroke wing. A secondary drawback is that because your opponent is answering your approach shot from the middle of the baseline, it is difficult for you to angle the volley away from him.

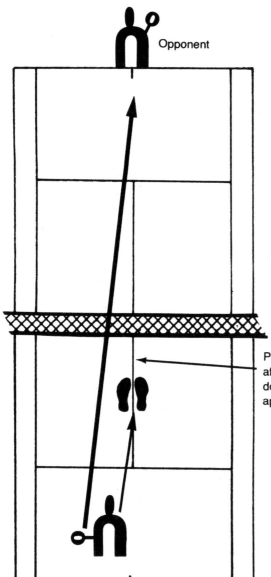

Opponent

Proper net position after hitting down-the-middle approach shot

Fig. 7.7   When you hit a backhand approach shot, it is often advisable to direct the ball down the middle of the court.

Angled approach shots. An obvious method of setting up an angled-volley putaway is to use the angled approach shot. This is also one of the most dangerous routes of approaching the net, since your opponent, in being angled, has an even greater angle open to him for his passing shot *(Fig. 7.8)*. In general, it is not a good idea to employ this approach shot.

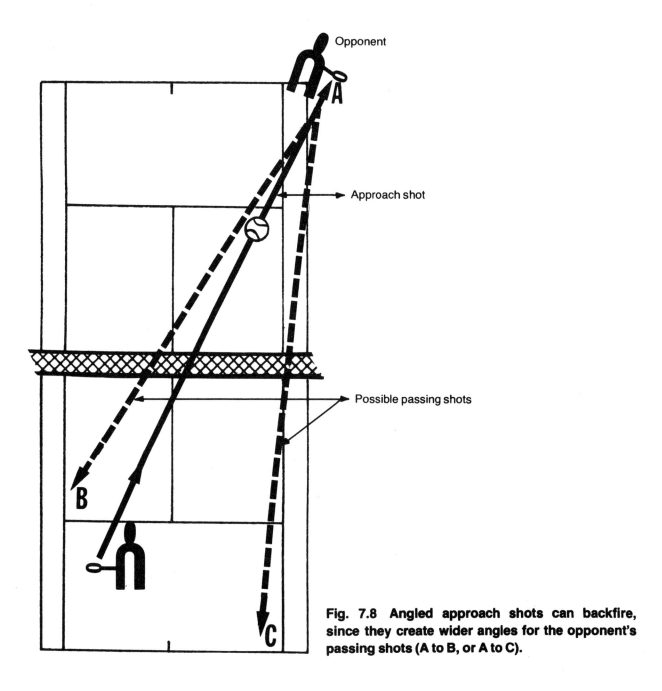

Opponent

A

Approach shot

Possible passing shots

B

C

Fig. 7.8 Angled approach shots can backfire, since they create wider angles for the opponent's passing shots (A to B, or A to C).

Low-and-short approach shots. You will discover that on clay courts there are speedy opponents who will skillfully lob or pass you after you hit a deep or angled approach shot. A possible answer to such a difficult opponent is an approach shot aimed low over the net, short, and near one of the sidelines. Although the lob will not be a threat to you after this approach shot, you must be concerned with passing shots. Some good players have the ability to handle this type of shot with overspin; others do not. Low, short approach shots to the backhand can result in many putaway volleys for you *(Fig. 7.9).*

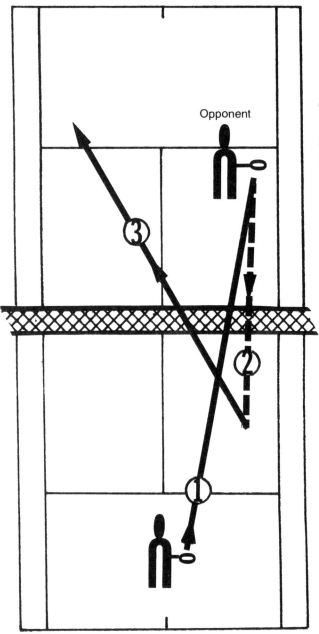

Opponent

Order of shots
1. Low, short approach shot
2. Ball is returned by opponent
3. Putaway volley is made

Fig. 7.9 The low and short approach shot to the opponent's backhand can be effective in opening the court for the putaway volley.

SHOULD YOU BE STATIONARY OR IN MOTION WHEN HITTING THE APPROACH SHOT?

This forcing shot can be hit in one of two ways: First, it can be stroked from a stationary position and then followed with a run to the net; this method affords maximum accuracy, and is almost a necessity for some two-handed hitters; second, approach shots can be hit while you are moving toward the forecourt. This technique enables you to advance closer to the net, where you can execute better volleys. Of the two methods, hitting the approach shot while in motion is more effective. Whether you come to a full stop before hitting or stroke the approach shot as you are moving, do not cease to concentrate on accuracy.

Since we must have good rhythm and a feel of the ball to make effective approach shots, it is often wise to get a game or two into the match before attempting them and advancing to the net. If you are especially eager to get a quick start against your opponent, it is advisable that you practice three or four approach shots in the warmup.

After hitting the approach shot, move to the net position as quickly as possible. Just as your opponent starts to hit his passing shot, pause, on your toes, assessing which direction to cover, and be sure to see you are set solidly at the moment you make your volley. Although the approach shot is often hit off an opponent's short, slow ball, it can be risky, since body movement is involved during or just after the shot.

The next member of the groundstroke family, the return of service, is difficult not because the body is moving but because the ball is coming at great speed. If you don't have adequate return of service, a good server will have a field day against you.

Chapter 8

RETURN-OF-SERVICE TACTICS

ARE YOU BREAKING SERVICE?

The major determinant of how well you are returning your opponent's service is the percentage of times you break his service (that is, the number of games he serves in which you win the game). Breaking service against a good serve-and-volleyer on a fast court is nearly impossible without an excellent return of service. On a slow (red) clay court with slow (European) balls, breaking the opponent's service is much less difficult, because unless his service is tremendous, the clay will act as an equalizer.

Change tactics if you are not breaking service. Since the receiver of service has a number of tactical options, it is advisable to change tactics if a particular type of return is not effective. The following are some of your return-of-service possibilities:

1. You can stand in front of or behind your baseline.
2. You can follow your return to the net or remain behind the baseline.
3. You can direct your returns closer to or farther from the lines or the net.
4. You can return the serve with or without spin.
5. You can return service hard or soft.
6. You can return serves crosscourt, down the line, or down the middle.

Your strategy will ultimately depend on your capabilities and those of your opponent.

Minimize return-of-service errors. It is important to remember that regardless of how strong your opponent's serve is, your most important objective is to get the ball back over the net. Your return of service, as much as any other shot, should be executed with the intention of forcing the opponent to *earn* his points throughout a match. Net rushers want you to feel pressure when they come to the net, but do not be hoodwinked into attempting low-percentage shots. Only when your opponent has proved to be an exceptional volleyer should you take more chances on your service returns.

Be aware of your return-of-service capabilities. As with all the other aspects of your game, you must have an awareness of your limitations in returning serve. Specifically, you must know how much ball control you have when returning hard, the lowest net clearance you can use safely to return service, how near the sidelines and the baseline you can aim, and how close to the net you can stand to return service accurately.

WHERE SHOULD YOU STAND TO RETURN SERVICE?

Standard receiving position. Most tournament players return service within three or four feet of the point where the baseline meets the singles sideline. Whenever the server assumes a radical position by moving away from the center mark, there must be a corresponding move by the receiver to compensate for this new angle *(Fig. 8.1)*.

Receiving service far in front of the baseline or far behind it. The main advantage of receiving service five to seven feet in front of the baseline is that the ball comes back to the server very quickly and allows him less time to react for his next shot. This tactic is especially effective against a serve-and-volleyer, as it prevents him from making his first volley close to the net. Returning a service early is also a good play when you want to attack a service and come to the net behind your return. And, standing in closer to the net is the most effective method of returning a high-bouncing American-twist service, since in this position you can cope with the spinning delivery at waist height rather than head height.

When you return service from five or six feet behind your baseline, you are allowed more time to prepare for the shot *(Fig. 8.2)*. Also, since the served ball slows down as it travels through the air, your chance of making an accurate return is greater than if you stood inside the baseline. Receiving service far behind the baseline affords the player with slower hands or reflexes the opportunity to make a solid return. However unless you can clobber a return with overspin, you cannot use this tactic on a regular basis against net rushers, since it allows them a volleying position too close to the net. Also you must be very alert to come up quickly for short, sharply angled serves.

Return-of-service positioning according to your stronger groundstroke. It is often a wise play to avoid your weak groundstroke and to return service on the side that is strongest and most consistent. It is advisable to develop a balanced game, not favoring one groundstroke or the other; nevertheless, after your game matures, you will almost surely have a forehand that is stronger than your backhand, or vice versa. Against a powerful and skillful server, avoiding a first

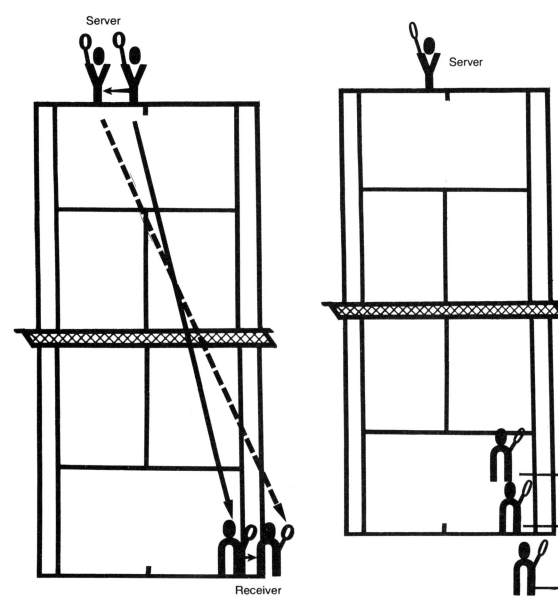

Server

Receiver

Server

Receiver's Positions
Receive high-bouncing twist serve here.
Receive most serves here.
Receive very hard serves here.

Fig. 8.1 When the server moves to a different position, the receiver must make a corresponding move.

Fig. 8.2 Move up or back according to the type of serve you receive.

service on one side or the other is very difficult. However, it is possible to hit most second serves with your strongest wing.

Return-of-service positioning according to the server's strength and his serving pattern. Some servers can serve well only to one of the corners of each service box. They have difficulty in hitting both corners on a regular basis. You, the receiver, should become aware of such a situation by making a mental note every time he serves an ace. For example, you should say to yourself, "He aced me wide to my forehand side when serving to the deuce court, so I'll be watching for this serve the next time."

An excellent tactic against the server who habitually hurts you by serving to the same place is to stand nearer that corner, making it impossible for him to ace you there *(Fig. 8.3)*. In addition to cutting off his effec-

tive serves, it usually forces him to serve more often to the corner of the service box where he is not grooved. (Tennis players instinctively hit toward openings, or uncovered areas of the court.) In other words, fake him out by not standing where you want him to aim his service. Positioning yourself in this manner can be psychologically upsetting even to an advanced or tournament player if he is unused to it. In essence you are telling the server, "You can hit a serve 150 miles an hour and place the ball right on the spot where the service line touches the singles sideline, and you won't get a clean ace. I will cover your effective primary target every time, unless you can show me you can hit the other corner of the service box. Only when you can prove to me that you can serve well to both corners will I stand in the normal receiving position."

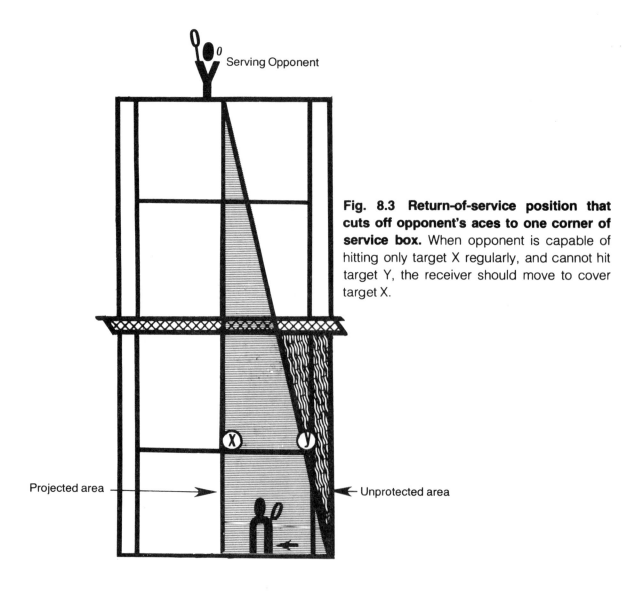

Fig. 8.3 Return-of-service position that cuts off opponent's aces to one corner of service box. When opponent is capable of hitting only target X regularly, and cannot hit target Y, the receiver should move to cover target X.

Return-of-service positioning and its disorientating of the server. Most players do not realize that the server uses the receiver as part of his "visual target." This is similar to the way a basketball player uses the net to zero in on the hoop. When the receiver moves to a radical position, away from the six-square-yard area he normally inhabits, he usually throws the server's perception slightly off. I have never seen a server who served his best when the receiver took an unorthodox return-of-service position.

On the other hand, the receiver often makes a tactical sacrifice when he takes unorthodox positions, such as just behind the service line, or fifteen feet behind the baseline, or near the center mark when the opponent is serving a second serve to the deuce court *(Fig. 8.4)*. Returning service from an unusual position will probably result in more errors by the receiver. Also, the receiver can be at a disadvantage on the next shot because of poor positioning.

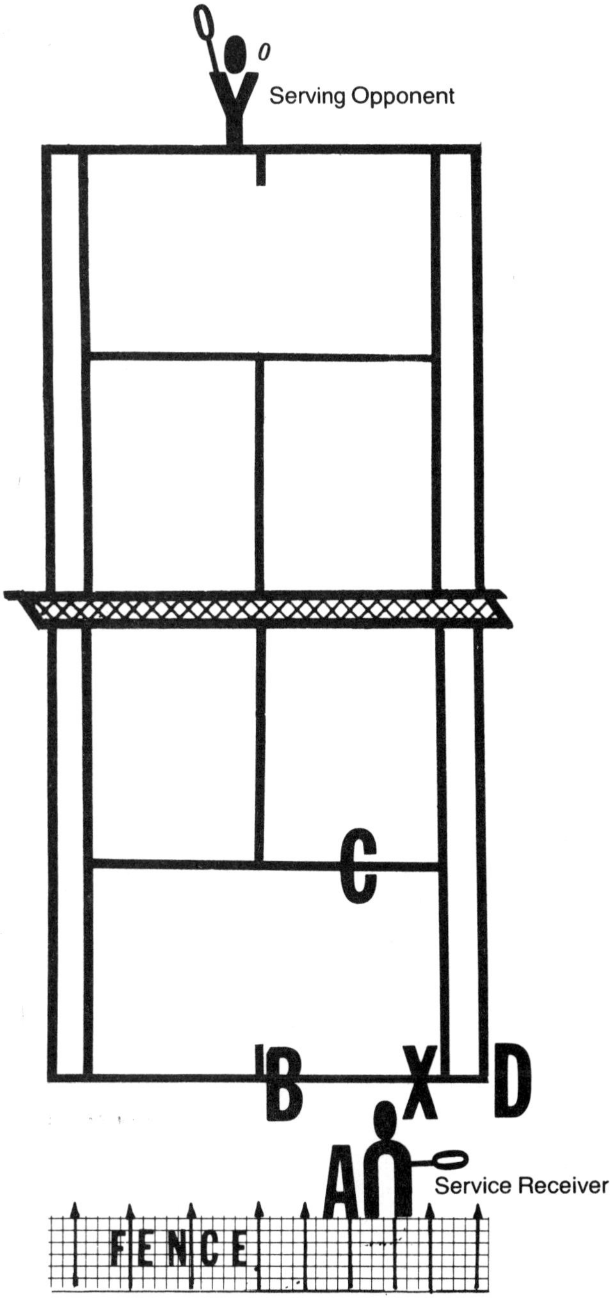

Serving Opponent

Fig. 8.4 Disorienting the server by taking an extreme position. When your serving opponent tosses the ball, you can move from these unorthodox positions (A, B, C, D) toward the normal receiving position (X).

C

B X D

A

Service Receiver

FENCE

55

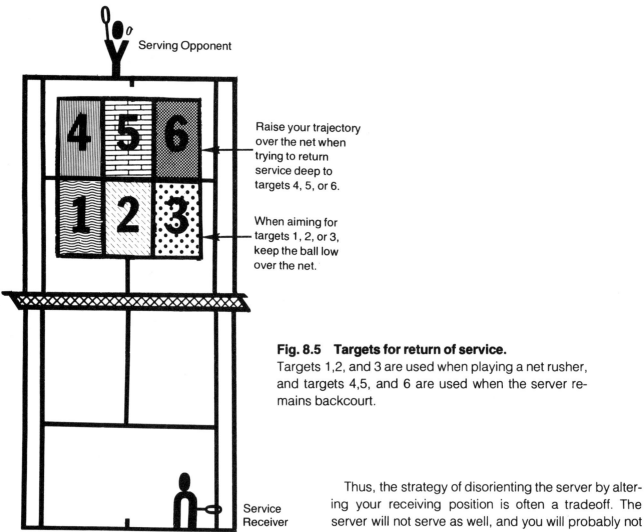

Serving Opponent

Raise your trajectory over the net when trying to return service deep to targets 4, 5, or 6.

When aiming for targets 1, 2, or 3, keep the ball low over the net.

Service Receiver

Fig. 8.5 Targets for return of service.
Targets 1, 2, and 3 are used when playing a net rusher, and targets 4, 5, and 6 are used when the server remains backcourt.

Thus, the strategy of disorienting the server by altering your receiving position is often a tradeoff. The server will not serve as well, and you will probably not return as well. Generally, it is best to try this against a big server when you are having difficulty breaking his service. It can also be an effective surprise tactic against other types of players. When using this play, try to concentrate doubly hard on returning the serve.

WHERE SHOULD YOU AIM YOUR RETURN OF SERVICE?

Essentially there are six places to aim when returning service either from the ad or the deuce court *(Fig. 8.5)*. If your opponent is rushing in after serving, you should keep your return low and near the net, forcing him to meet the ball as near the ground as possible. You can make the net rusher stretch wide *(targets 1 and 3),* or direct the ball right at him. Against the serving net rusher who blankets the net, often your best bet is *not* to direct the ball out of his reach, as you may err wide of the sideline.

When the server stays back on his service, you obviously want to keep your ball as deep in the court as possible. In this case you will aim for a slightly higher return than you would if your opponent served and volleyed.

The direction of your service return depends on the strength of the server's forehand and backhand groundstrokes and his volley as well as your own strengths. For example, if you are in the ad court and your backhand return of service is much better down the line than crosscourt, use this tactic most of the time. If your serving opponent has a much stronger forehand than backhand volley, you might give nine returns in ten to his backhand side. When he senses you do not respect a particular stroke of his, he can become very unnerved.

MOVING TOWARD THE NET AFTER EXECUTING A LOW RETURN TO THE NET RUSHER.

An advanced and effective play against a serve-and-volleyer is to return the ball low over the net and near the sideline (targets 1 and 3 in Fig. 8.5) and to follow with an advance to the net. In most cases you will not be able to reach your service line before answering his first volley. However, there is a chance you can minimize the effect of his volley attack by using this strategy.

By following your return of service to the net you often force him to alter his volleying pattern. He will not be allowed to hit medium-speed, safe volleys toward one of the corners, since you will be in a position to intercept them. Against this tactic he will often be forced to hit short angled volleys, a play he may not like to make. This return strategy can be used now and then as a surprise tactic.

Moving in after your return of service is especially effective on cement, grass, or a carpetlike synthetic surface. Ranking California tournament players who have been brought up on cement are especially adept at executing this play. This is one of the few instances in tennis in which playing a ball or two from "no-man's-land" can pay dividends.

WHAT TYPES OF SHOTS SHOULD YOU USE ON RETURN OF SERVICE?

Against a net rusher, an *overspin* return of service is by far the most effective. A topspin return can cause a net rusher to have to volley at his shoetops when he is as close as twelve or thirteen feet from the net. The kind of spin you use against the player who stays back on his service is not particularly important.

Flat returns are not as effective, since they do not dip below the level of the net, as overspins do, and they often go over the baseline because there is no spin to pull them down in the court. The advantage of the flat return, however, is that the ball comes back to the server quickly, and he will not have as much time to advance as close to the net as he could against a slower, undercut ball.

The *sliced* return of service is usually ineffective when playing a good net rusher unless it is hit early (i.e. on the rise) and passes very low over the net. Since a slice rises after racket contact, it becomes an easy ball to volley away unless it has unusually vicious spin, which can trouble a volleyer.

The *hard* return of service, regardless of whether it is hit flat or with spin, is more effective against the net rusher than one softly hit. In addition to allowing him less time to gain good volleying position, it frequently causes the volleyer to mistime the ball. Mixing in an occasional soft return with a hard one can also upset a net rusher's timing.

As a last resort against a skillful serve-and-volleyer, the *lob* can be used to try to slow down his dash to the net. Although it is not a good percentage tactic under ordinary circumstances, if you are not breaking service, you have little to lose by trying to lob a service return. In the highly publicized final of the 1963 U.S. Open, at Forest Hills, Raphael Osuna used lob returns of service against Frank Froehling III. Osuna was standing twenty to thirty feet behind the baseline when he used this play. At other times he returned Froehling's thunderous service from a normal position. Osuna's feathery touch on the lob and his catlike quickness afoot were prerequisites for this unusual tactic. Osuna, the fine Mexican sportsman, won the match. The tennis world lost his talents prematurely when he died in an airplane crash.

The *drop shot* can be an effective return-of-service tactic against a slow server who does not rush the net. It is easiest to execute when returning a second service. After drop-shotting the service, it can be advantageous to come to the net. This depends on how low over the net your shot goes, and whether or not your opponent is able to overspin a low and short ball.

It is important to develop a return of service that you block back, as well as one you can attack with. The *block* return must be used against big servers because there is little time for a backswing. When blocking a return of service, do not intentionally take your racket behind you; simply turn your shoulders, and this will automatically give you a short backswing. Have your weight going forward on all returns. The attacking return of service is usually made with a longer backswing and with overspin. Practice returning a few of your opponent's serves in a conservative, or blocking, manner before hitting them hard. Try to synchronize your movements with his service rhythm in the warm-up.

ATTACKING A SECOND (OR SLOW) SERVICE

One component of a top returning game is the ability to "cream" a slow second service. The following are the main reasons why this aggressive return-of-service skill should be developed:

1. When you hit a return of service with great pace, you can win points either on outright placements or on the opponent's errors. Extremely hard returns extract errors from the volleyer even when the ball is aimed directly to him.
2. Returning a service with sizzling pace can force the server to hit harder than usual, which could result in double faults.
3. Successfully attacking a player's second serve often forces him to slow down his first service so as to achieve a higher first-service percentage and avoid a second-service attack. (This can also have a marked effect on his morale.)
4. If you have the ability to lace into a second service with accuracy, you can prevent anyone besides an exceptional second-server from sustaining a continuous serve-and-volley attack.

Remember that a hard and deep service is difficult to attack. However, a slow, shallow service is the perfect ball to hit for an approach shot. Just as you attack a ball landing in your service box during a normal exchange, you should be offensive on the return of service as well, whenever you get the opportunity.

WATCHING THE SERVER'S TOSS FOR CLUES TO SPIN AND DIRECTION

Some players telegraph their serves by the manner in which they toss the ball. Most of the time you should know when a big twist or a slice is coming at you even before your serving opponent strikes the ball. A few top international players will disguise the spin and direction of their serves by making all service tosses to one spot, but this is difficult to do. You will also discover that when the service action is fast, there is much less time to "read" the server.

An *American-twist* service toss is usually placed farther to the server's left (receiver's right) than other tosses. In addition, it is usually tossed farther behind the server than the normal, flat-service toss. Also, a twist involves a bending or arching of the server's back. When a twist is coming toward you, move forward and slightly to your left *(Fig. 8.6)*. By doing this, you will be able to receive the ball at a comfortable height rather than at an awkwardly high level.

Fig. 8.6 This toss indicates the American-twist service.
Normal service toss
American-twist service toss

A *heavily sliced* service has a toss that is to the server's right *(receiver's left) (Fig. 8.7)*. The receiver should move to his right when he is receiving this serve. Bobby Riggs used this serve effectively against Margaret Court in their nationally televised "battle of the sexes" match. Since Riggs has a slow and deliberate serving action, the TV viewer could see it coming long before it was actually delivered.

Fig. 8.7   This toss indicates a heavily sliced service.
Normal service toss
Heavily sliced service toss

In order to return service well and to force yourself to concentrate on the server's toss, try using the two-count method. Say "one" to yourself as you look at the ball your opponent tosses to serve, and "two" as you focus on the ball coming toward you.

DEVELOPING YOUR RETURN OF SERVICE

To perfect a top return of service, you must practice against a variety of good servers, including those with left-handed slices, heavy twists, and bullet serves. Spending a lot of time practicing returns of service on fast courts is especially valuable.

Your primary purpose when receiving service should be to try to return the ball. Then, once you're able to return nearly all serves somewhere in the court, try to negate the server's advantage by placing the ball where he cannot attack you successfully. The third and final objective of the return of service is to be able to put the server on the defensive, and to have a strategic advantage after making the return. Don Budge, Lew Hoad, Rod Laver, and Jimmy Connors have been and are great return-of-service artists.

THE ULTIMATE RETURN OF SERVICE

It is my belief that great returns of service can be made from a position about halfway between the baseline and the service line. Serves that lack depth can be decisively taken advantage of by returning from this position.

When returning service from a few feet behind the service line, you will gain an advantage over the server if you are able to make a hard and solid drive. The direction of your return of service is almost a secondary factor if the ball is well hit. But when the return is mishit, the probability of your winning the point is lessened. It is very difficult for beginners or intermediates to return serves from far inside the baseline.

Why is this "close-in" return effective? You make it almost impossible for a net-rushing server to attain good forecourt position by denying him sufficient time to do so. Also, by returning service from here, you can take excellent net position yourself.

A deep serve landing in the corner of the service box is a challenge to return from this shallow position. With steady practice it is possible for a highly skilled player to develop this technique.

We have covered the return of service, which is an essential shot in tennis. The groundstroke described in the next chapter is optional, and can be used effectively only by those players who have mastered it. Those who do not have the ability to execute an accurate drop shot often play match after match absorbing punishment, without being able to give some in return.

Chapter

DROP-SHOT TACTICS

WHY DO WE HIT DROP SHOTS?

Although a drop-shot attempt can be a losing proposition for many players, it can be used with deadly effect by touch artists who know when to use it on a clay court. There are three main advantages to the drop shot:

1. *You can win points either by making clean winners or by causing your opponent to err.* The drop shot breaks your opponent's rhythm, and can dislodge a steady backcourt opponent from a grooved groundstroke pattern.

   The periodic use of an effective drop shot offers the element of surprise. The opponent must keep his anticipation honed so that he can detect at the earliest possible moment whether you intend to execute a drive or a drop shot.

   Even if your opponent returns your drop shot, you can often follow it up with a lob or a passing shot. The drop-shot victim is not capable of changing direction quickly to prepare for the next shot.

2. *A drop shot tires the opponent by forcing him to sprint fast and far.* The drop shot also prevents him from relaxing during rallies.

3. *With the threat of an effective drop shot, you can prevent your rival from venturing far behind his baseline.* When a player is allowed to position himself regularly nine or ten feet behind his baseline, he can minimize groundstroke errors. Although we intentionally try to keep the good volleyer well behind his baseline, there are some groundstrokers who have great looping shots, and against them we should employ the drop shot. It forces them to the forecourt, where they are less effective.

WHOM SHOULD WE DROP-SHOT?

Since tough drop shots are painfully punishing, they can be especially effective against the poorly conditioned athlete in hot weather. The mediocre volleyer is another good drop-shot victim because you can bring him to a part of the court where he is ineffective. The immobile or slow-footed player is susceptible to the drop shot for obvious reasons. A soft-ball hitter is an ideal candidate to receive the drop shot because he gives you the perfect ball to drop-shot with accuracy. Finally, a two-handed-backhand player can be vulnerable to a drop shot since it often forces him to slice, and can necessitate a one-handed shot. It is difficult for some players to slice using the two-handed backhand.

Conversely, the worst candidate to drop shot against is the quick cat who has great touch and angling ability. A fleet-footed player will often turn your own drop shot against you.

The drop shot–lob combination can be a point maker against the smaller player whose reach is limited. When the short person is a great leaper such as former Wimbledon champion Chuck McKinley, it is best to forget this ploy.

WHEN AND WHEN NOT TO DROP-SHOT

When you are playing on a clay court, the drop shot can be very effective because foot traction is poor and the ball will usually be moving slowly enough for you to make a fine touch shot. There are a few instances in which the drop shot is effective on hard courts, such as in super-senior-division play, in young boys' and girls' matches, and in women's play.

Balls that are soft and slow are easier to drop-shot than very firm balls. Since new balls play faster than used ones, it is often advisable not to drop-shot until the balls are less lively.

Since the drop shot requires touch, it is wise to wait until you have proper timing before employing this stroke. Gaining proper rhythm and timing on an opponent's ball usually requires a few minutes of play. It is advisable not to drop-shot toward the end of a tough match, because at this stage pressure is mounting, and you may not have the proper touch.

Although it is generally best not to overuse the drop shot and thus lose the element of surprise, I have seen it used on clay as much as two or three times a game with great effectiveness. The more drop shots a player strokes within a given period, the more consistent his delivery becomes.

A drop shot should be attempted from inside the baseline. If the shot is executed from the baseline or from behind the baseline, the opponent is given too much time to retrieve the ball. When you are in a position to drop-shot, you will have the opportunity to hit an approach shot as well. Luis Ayala, of Chile, developed identical backswings for both his drop shot and his approach shot, and it was suicidal for his opponent to give him a short ball.

Drop-shot your opponent when he is behind his baseline, so that he is forced to run a great distance to retrieve the shot. You should also disguise this shot by stepping toward the net before contacting the ball, as you would on a normal stroke. When you do this, your opponent, anticipating a drive, will probably lean slightly backward and will be more vulnerable to the drop shot.

An excellent time to attempt a drop shot is during a crosscourt rally from forehand to forehand or from backhand to backhand. In this case you would aim your drop shot down the line *(Fig. 9.1).*

Another time to utilize this stroke is when you have an opponent who runs around his backhand ground-stroke, taking it with the forehand; his forehand side is then susceptible to a drop shot. Adriano Panatta, the fine Italian player, has used this strategy successfully. *(Fig. 9.2).*

Fig. 9.1 Drop shot after deep crosscourt exchange.

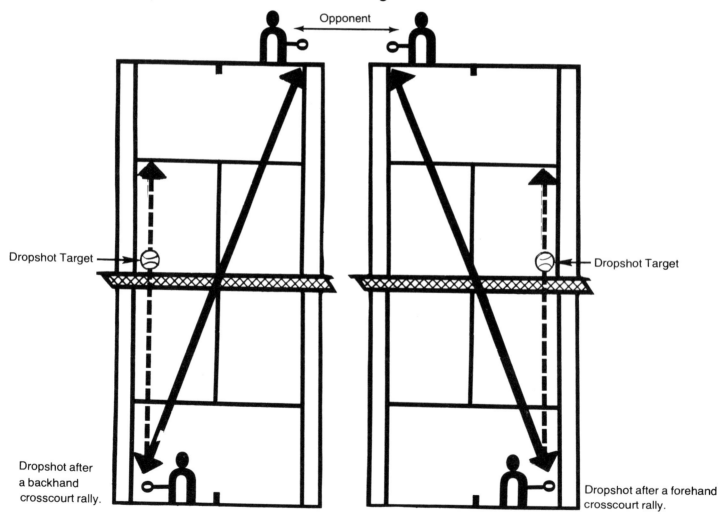

Opponent

Dropshot Target

Dropshot Target

Dropshot after a backhand crosscourt rally.

Dropshot after a forehand crosscourt rally.

If you cannot slice balls from the back of the court or even when volleying at the net, mastering the drop shot will indeed be difficult. Since all underspin shots are of the same family, the use of one develops and strengthens the use of another.

Hitting drop shots is usually more difficult for the player who uses a steel or even an aluminum racket. Some composite rackets have great "touch"; however, wood is still my favorite for execution of the drop shot as well as the lob. Yes, Jimmy Connors uses steel, but he is virtually alone among the world-class stars in this respect.

HOW AND WHERE SHOULD WE DROP-SHOT?

The most important component of a good drop shot is a short and fast racket action, to prevent detection. Since smaller players can execute the drop shot more quickly than their bigger counterparts, they are usually more effective. The drop shot should be stroked with adequate backspin, to slow down its forward motion, and ideally it should clear the net by no more than two feet. A good drop shot must land as close to the net as possible, and it is usually hit to the opponent's backhand side.

You should be aware of the great degree of risk in executing the drop shot. For many players, it is a low-percentage shot. As you are learning, you should play the shot safely, using little racket head speed, and not hitting too close to the net. Even with a relatively safe drop shot you can gain the upper hand in the point (Fig. 9.3).

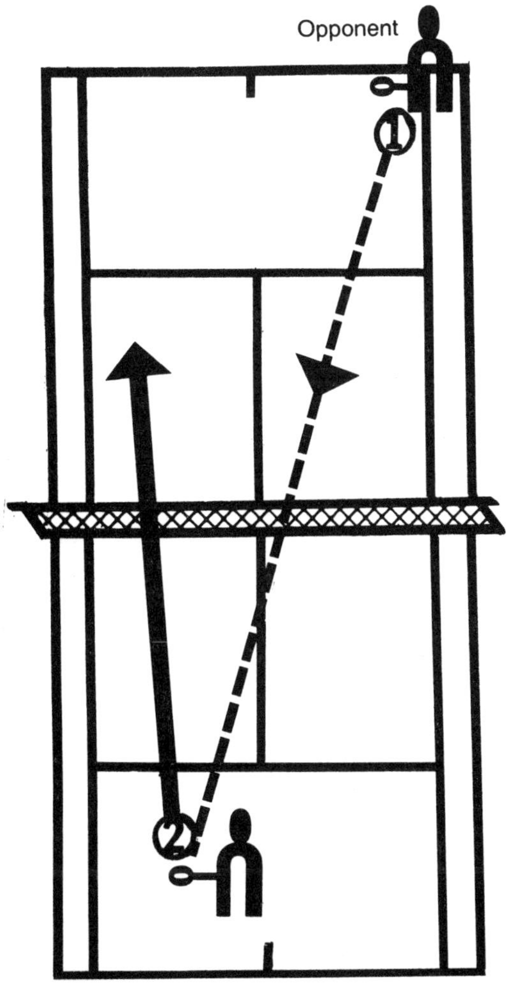

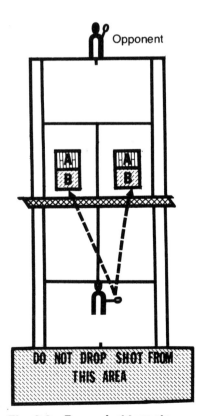

A. Target for safe drop shot (brings opponent to net)
B. Target for drop-shot winner

Fig. 9.2 Drop-shotting to the open court is a good tactic against opponent who runs around backhand and uses forehand.

Fig. 9.3 Drop-shot targets

If you have made a great drop shot, it is usually wise to follow it to the net, since any volley of the return will likely produce a winner. If you do come to the net behind your drop shot, and cannot volley the ball past the opponent for a winner, be ready to lob volley, providing you have this advanced shot in your repertoire.

DROP-SHOT DEFENSE

Opposing a gifted drop-shot artist is an unenviable experience, to put it mildly. You will get jerked and bounced around the court as if you were on your first ride on a roller coaster. You will have to work unbelievably hard if the opponent hits drop shots with regularity.

Such a master of the drop shot was Ramanathan Krishnan, of India, who defeated nearly every top player in the world when he was at his peak. (He was given a prestigious world's-top-ten ranking for four years.) Krishnan had a style of his own that included an unorthodox open-stance backhand groundstroke that was incredibly accurate. He could run his opponents unmercifully with the drop shot. Watching him in 1962, on the clay courts at the Dutch championships, I saw victim after victim come off the court with bloody knees after wildly chasing his touch shots around the court. His tactics resembled an organ grinder's controlling a monkey on a chain. However, in the championship match of that tournament, Rod Laver handled Krishnan. The great depth and pace of Laver's shots thwarted Krishnan's attempts to establish his torturous drop-shot game. If you find yourself being hurt by an opponent's drop shots, use tactics like those of Laver, and try to lengthen your groundstrokes, and hit a little harder. If the opponent has an accurate drop shot, you may have either to play most of the points from on or inside the baseline or to start a net attack.

Another answer to a drop shot is to drop-shot in return. This can be difficult, however, since you probably will be off balance when you reach the ball. In most cases your best return is down-the-line and deep. You can also hit a drop shot directly back to your opponent if he remains on his baseline.

When you are playing a touch artist, pay close attention to the pattern of his drop shots. For example, if he tends to drop-shot short, soft balls hit to his backhand side, move in a step or two after you direct the ball there. In this instance watch for him to cock his elbow just before he strokes.

If you are not fully confident of the drop shot, do not use it in important matches. Many players attempt this stroke when they should not. Learn the drop shot by using it on insignificant points in nontournament matches. The backboard is excellent for developing the drop shot because you can hit as many as twenty strokes in a minute. Your practice efforts will pay dividends if you can incorporate this shot into your game. If you have mastered the drop shot, you can use it with devastating effect, especially on clay.

Although the drop shot is an important weapon to possess, it is not essential. There have been a few great players who did not use a drop shot. However, a particular ability that all good players must possess is discussed in the next three chapters. This is the skill to cope with the eternal menace: the net rusher.

Chapter 10

TACTICS AGAINST A NET RUSHER

When you are facing a tough serve-and-volleyer, you will realize that the outcome of nearly every point, and of the match, is largely in his hands. *He* usually makes the shot (volley or overhead smash), or misses it. When the net-rushing opponent is tall and agile, and you are playing on a fast court, your job of coping with him becomes doubly difficult. The pressure that a young Pancho Gonzales or a Jack Kramer could apply was incredible. (Kramer never lost a career-long head-to-head series with anyone on the pro tour.) The match was completely out of the backcourter's control.

Bill Tilden was over-stating, in my opinion, when he stated that the answer to any net-rushing attack is in powerful and accurate groundstrokes. On slow clay courts this can be the case, but considering the great number of fast surfaces in the world today, primarily of asphalt base, the serve-and-volleyer usually has the advantage.

Although Gonzales and Kramer were almost invincible on fast courts, with their power and their long reach, the situation against the average net rusher is not quite so hopeless. There are a number of players who come to the net yet do not actually have a reliable volley or smash. They advance to the net for two main reasons: one, they have watched tournament-tennis players attack and have read that this is a desirable tactic; two, they expect (often rightfully so) that their opponents will succumb to their bluff, and overhit the passing shot.

Do not be bluffed by the net rusher. As explained in the chapter on return of service, the message that the net rusher tries to send you is that since *he* is at the net, *you,* in the backcourt, must hit a special shot in order to win the point. For the average player, it is wise just to keep the ball in play and make him earn his points.

If the opponent is coming to the net and losing more points there than in the back of his court, you want him to continue coming in. However, if he is coming to the net and winning the majority of points, then you must

try to keep him away from the barrier by denying him easy balls to approach on. If an opponent is coming to the net behind his good service, there is nothing you can do to deter him besides making tougher returns of service.

TACTICAL PLAYS TO USE AGAINST THE GOOD VOLLEYER-SMASHER

Following are some of the strategic options you can use against the tough net rusher:

1. You yourself can serve and volley, and at least have the net position fifty percent of the time. (Sometimes, however, the skillful net rusher will take the net even on your own serve.)

2. When your sharp-volleying opponent is in the back of his court, you should hit your baseline shots as deep and hard as possible. (If you hit with depth, but not with pace, the capable net rusher will often intercept the shot as a volley and come into the forecourt.) By hitting penetrating groundstrokes, and serving with depth and pace, you make it difficult for the aggressive player to come to the net and volley with accuracy. He will more likely miss his approach shots, and will not be able to gain good forecourt position close to the net.

3. If the opponent is advancing to the net off your service, place it wide, both to the deuce and the ad courts, to make him come up to the net from an angle. (The net man will have his body weight going partially sideways as he comes in to volley, and this will result in less net coverage and a greater number of errors off his racket.)

4. Since net rushing is usually more strenuous than playing from the back of the court, there are a few instances when you should allow, and even encourage, him to come to the forecourt. (On slow courts, rushing the net on the majority of points can be taxing physically. On hot days an

inexperienced net rusher can expend so much energy that he can put himself out of a match even after winning the first set.)

The net rusher who suffers the heaviest physical toll is one who rushes in very fast, and moves to a position extremely close to the net. Those volleyers who operate out of the midcourt area work very little in comparison.

There is one net-rushing stylist who will make you, the baseliner, run and work harder than he. This is the player who angle-volleys short and away from his opponent. (This style will be discussed in detail in Chapter 14.)

5. Almost always lob if the volleyer is close enough to the net to take one step and touch it with his racket. Hit a passing shot or a dink whenever the opponent is in volleying position farther than twelve feet from the net. (A worthwhile exercise to develop this habit is listed in my book *Tennis Drills*.)

This chapter was concerned with your alternatives when confronted by a net rusher. The following chapter deals with passing-shot and dink tactics, which you can use once the opponent is entrenched at the net.

Chapter 11

PASSING-SHOT AND DINK TACTICS

Play within your capabilities. This first bit of advice on using passing shots in match play applies to your other strokes as well. Do not attempt low-percentage shots. It is in practice matches that we should use shots which we have not fully mastered. In tournament play, or in important practice matches with better players, use only those strokes and plays you know are reliable. For example, if your big topspin down-the-line backhand taken on the rise goes in the court only one out of three times, do not use it when the chips are down; continue to develop this stroke through drilling and backboard workouts. You must know the accuracy of your down-the-lines compared with your cross-courts, and how your hard shots compare with your soft ones.

The better your net-rushing opponent is, the more chances you should take. Hit passing shots only as close to the lines as is necessary. Against a good tournament-level volleyer, keep your passing shots low, near the sidelines, and preferably with topspin. You must also hit quickly. Otherwise, your opponent will have a field day. Against a poor volleyer it is not worth the gamble to hit quickly and very low.

You should know your opponent's strengths and weaknesses at the net. Is his forehand volley weaker than his backhand volley? Does he tend to aim his volleys to one place, or does he vary their direction? How well does he handle pace, or the lack of it?

Do not feel you must try to pass him on the first ball. Sometimes the best play is not to attempt a hard passing shot on the first ball you receive. In many instances you will want to hit a dink (low and soft slice) or a slow topspin drive on the first shot, and perhaps on the second and third, hoping to extract a ball that you can time for a solid passing shot. Unless you have a good opening for a passing shot, try to maneuver your opponent out of position. By engaging net rushers in practice, you will have the opportunity to try this plan of percentage placement and will have less of a tendency to panic in matches.

WHAT SHOULD BE THE DIRECTION OF YOUR PASSING SHOTS?

First of all, when the ball is coming at you, you must decide very early, and firmly, exactly what kind of shot you are going to hit and where you will direct the ball; otherwise, your attempted passing shot will likely result in an error.

Racket preparation for the passing shot. I have found it best to set my feet and shoulders for the down-the-line passing shot regardless of whether I am aiming there or crosscourt. This will prevent hesitancy from interfering with your stroke preparation. It also prevents experienced volleyers from reading the direction of your shot by your body preparation. A short explosive backswing is more difficult to read than a longer one.

Crosscourt passing shots. As was stated earlier, there is more safety in the crosscourt shot because of the lower net and longer diagonal court. A dink from the backhand is best directed crosscourt because it is easier to keep the ball low and, in addition, it is more difficult for the opponent to put the ball away for a winner.

Down-the-line passing shots. The big advantage of the down-the-line passing shot is that it reaches the net, and thus the volleyer, more quickly than the crosscourt, and thus gives the net man less time to react. The down-the-line overspin passing shot is also advantageous because the ball will "curve" slightly around the net man (*Fig. 11.1*). Naturally, the down-the-line shot is slightly more of a risk than the crosscourt because the top of the net is higher at the sides than in the center.

Aiming directly at the volleyer. There are a few volleyers who, after you hit at an angle and make them reach wide, will direct their shots back at an even greater angle. Against this type of player, you can try hitting a very hard groundstroke directly at him, especially when you are near the net, moving, and hitting a

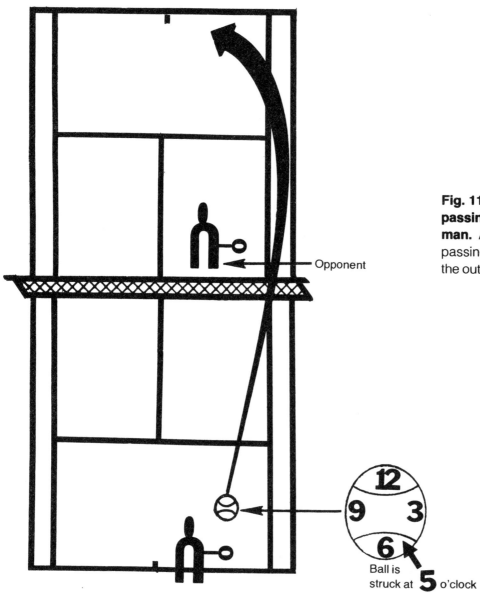

Opponent

Fig. 11.1 "Curving" a forehand passing shot around the net man. An excellent down-the-line passing shot is hit with topspin on the outside of the ball.

Ball is
struck at **5** o'clock

low ball. Certainly, if you do hit your opponent, you will follow up with an apology.

The crucial determining factors in passing-shot direction are your strengths and weaknesses as against those of your opponent. Unless your opponent has a glaring weakness, mix up the direction of your passing shots so he will be unable to anticipate them.

INGREDIENTS OF A PASSING SHOT

Net clearance. The most difficult passing shot for the volleyer to handle is the ball that is hit hard and skims low over the net (*Fig. 11.2*). When the net man is forced to volley a very low ball, it is difficult for him to hit the volley hard, or to angle it well, for fear of hitting the net.

Fig. 11.2 Net clearance for passing and other types of shots. Keep passing shots low.
Passing shots
Regular shots
Loops
Lobs

To develop the ability to hit low passing shots, be sure to concentrate on this while engaging in the most trivial warming-up session. When your opponent is practicing volleys, and you are behind the baseline, keep the ball low. If you make any errors, be certain they are of the kind where the ball hits the top of the net rather than going beyond the baseline. The only exception to this would be in the case of a beginner playing a match with another player on his level. He should try not to make any errors, even if it means clearing the net by four feet and directing his shot right at the net player. Beginning-level baseliners should have very little to fear when faced with beginning volleyers.

Spin on passing shots. Topspin passing shots are by far the best since they drop quickly to a very low point on the other side of the net. The volleyer is forced to hit up, in a defensive manner. A hard topspin shot is a difficult ball to judge because it drops quickly. A player who hits with topspin on all of his backcourt shots (no slices, sidespins, or flat ones) has an advantage in hitting passing shots since, in actuality, he is constantly grooving them. Eastern grips (not Continental or Australian) are advantageous when hitting overspin passing shots. Passing shots should not be sliced (*Fig. 11.3*).

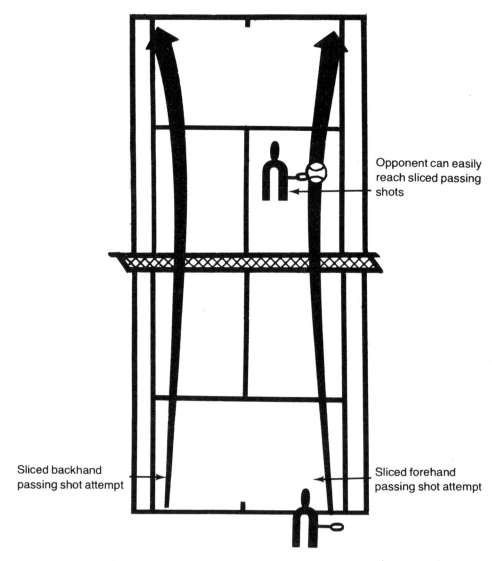

Opponent can easily reach sliced passing shots

Sliced backhand passing shot attempt

Sliced forehand passing shot attempt

Fig. 11.3 Do not slice passing shots, because
1) if the volleyer cannot touch them they will curve outside of the court
2) they will travel through the air too slowly, and
3) they rise in the air, making them easy to volley.

Hard versus soft passing shots. It is imperative that we allow the net man as little time as possible to get set for his volleys; this is one of the baseliner's few defenses. Hard passing shots accomplish this, and create timing problems as well. In his big Las Vegas match with Rod Laver, Jimmy Connors was occasionally hitting passing shots so hard that even when they went directly to Laver, Connors would often extract an error. When a ball is hit with tremendous speed, even an accurate volleyer will make errors. Some baseline artists prefer to hit very hard shots when their opponent is at the net, but will not take chances by placing the ball out of the net man's reach within a foot or two of the sideline.

A soft and low passing shot can, periodically, be a good play. Naturally, there is less risk involved than with a hard drive. Simply because of gravity, a soft ball drops relatively quickly, even when undercut. The soft passing shot is an excellent change of pace, and will make your hard shots more effective in comparison.

The soft passing shot is also a sound play against the volleyer who does not close in on the net quickly. The intelligent use of the soft passing shot affords the baseliner greater opportunity to regain balance and court position than if he had attempted a hard one.

Taking the passing shot early or late. Again, let me emphasize the importance of not allowing the net man a lot of time to intercept your passing shot. The more time he has, the closer to the net he will advance and the better balanced he will be. If you stand five feet or more behind your baseline, you allow him too much time to reach your passing shot. Try to hit passing shots from no more than two feet behind your baseline.

By taking a position on the baseline or inside it, you will be forced to hit the ball either at its peak or as it is rising from the bounce. If you are thinking of developing a very strong game, you must avoid hitting the passing shot after the ball has reached its maximum height. As a beginner or lower intermediate, it will be very difficult for you to hit passing shots on the rise. Develop this very advanced stroke as you improve.

MOVEMENT AFTER HITTING PASSING SHOTS

Since most volleyers will aim their shots toward the open court, it is advisable to move in that direction immediately after you hit your passing shot. When you find yourself hopelessly offcourt, move a step or two in the direction of the obvious opening, and then stop. If he hits the ball to where he thinks you will not be, he will be mistaken, and you will be balanced and ready for the shot. It is your speed afoot or lack of it, as much as anything else, that determines your ability to cope with a tough volleyer.

Be alert to your opponent's volleying patterns. For example, if he tends to drop-volley a considerable number of times off the forehand, start moving slightly toward the net when you give him a forehand volley.

Sound passing shots are important, but you can never deter a top-notch net rusher unless you bring one more weapon into play—the lob. A finely placed lob is extremely difficult for the net man to deal with, and is the subject of the next chapter.

Chapter **12**

LOBBING TACTICS

The lob plays a key role in thwarting the attack of a net rusher. We cannot have a formidable defense without a good lob.

WHY DO WE LOB?

1. The lob keeps the good volleyer from taking a position close to the net.
2. You can tire your opponent by forcing him to smash lobs. There is no shot in tennis that requires so much effort as the overhead smash, which is the response to the lob. Some experienced clay-court players will send up ten or twelve lobs early in a match to "soften up" an opponent. On hot days on slow courts, lobs can frustrate an opponent. If the smasher is sweating profusely, his problem will be compounded.
3. You can regain better court position by using high lobs.
4. Low-trajectory lobs can win points outright, and all lobs can produce errors from the opponent.
5. When there is a bright sun, the lob is effective in producing errors from the smasher.
6. If your opponent has a good volley, but a poor overhead smash, you can keep him from the net by lobbing.

A few years ago there was a capable California tennis pro named Bill Parks who played various U.S. tournaments. His best results were on clay courts, where he had wins over some of the top thirty players in the U.S. Parks had excellent groundstrokes but lacked a serve and had an almost nonexistent overhead smash. Another Californian, Bert Brown, who was a masseur–circuit player, knew Parks's weakness and would beat him by drop-shotting and then lobbing him. After they played, Parks would come off the court disgusted. "Drop shot, drop shot, drop shot—lob, lob, lob," he could cry at the end of a match. Although Brown was good, he was incapable of beating some

of the international-class players that Parks could; however, he was an expert in capitalizing on Parks's weakness. Parks needed one of Brown's rubdowns after being victimized by his tiring tactics on the court.

WHAT ARE THE BEST CONDITIONS FOR LOBBING?

1. High temperature and high humidity.
2. Slow courts and slow balls.
3. When the opponent lacks a firm and accurate overhead (check his overhead during the warm-up).
4. When the opponent is in poor physical condition.
5. When there is bright, glaring sunshine.

THE TWO KINDS OF LOBS

Offensive lob. This is a low-trajectory lob aimed a foot or two above the net man's maximum reach. It is usually executed from inside the baseline. When stroking an offensive lob you are hoping for either an outright winner or a defensive return that you can hit past the net man for a winning shot.

The offensive lob is most effective when used in the following three situations:

1. When the opponent is within six feet of the net. When he is this close to the barrier, you should lob almost every time (*Fig. 12.1*).
2. When the opponent is quickly rushing toward the net.
3. When the opponent does not have the athletic ability to leap quickly and smash.

The offensive lob should be disguised as a passing shot until the last second, at which time the racket head should be dropped and the shot executed. This lob should be aimed over the opponent's backhand side (*see Fig. 12.1*), since perhaps only one tournament player in ten is capable of putting away a backhand smash on a slow court. The offensive lob should be directed as deep as possible within the court. Bobby Riggs had an uncanny lob that helped account for many of his wins, including a tour victory over Don Budge.

Fig. 12.1 Lob almost every ball when the opponent is very close to the net (because volleys are seldom missed here).

The low-trajectory forehand lob is ordinarily hit with some overspin, whereas backhands are usually undercut. The overspin-backhand lob can be very effective, but is exceedingly difficult to master and requires infinite precision. Very few tournament players are capable of stroking this shot with consistency. An excellent time to use the overspin lob is when you are two or three feet behind the baseline and are being forced wide offcourt. It is advisable to overspin lobs crosscourt rather than down the line because of the extra court length. Manuel Santana, the gifted Spanish player, had an excellent overspin lob that would often trap opposing net rushers.

An offensive lob can also be effective when the opponent is in the back of his court; in this case it is referred to as a "loop," as described in Chapter 6.

Defensive lob. This lob is used when you are in poor court position, deep behind the baseline (five to twenty feet). Here a passing shot is unfeasible because of the distance the ball must travel. A long-distance passing-shot attempt can easily be cut off by the net man. A defensive lob is usually made when the baseliner's weight is going away from the net, thus making a powerful passing shot impossible from behind the baseline. This lob can also be used as a method of obtaining a brief rest if you are being run unmercifully by an opponent's side-to-side groundstrokes.

The defensive lob should be aimed as high as possible, since the higher the ball goes, the faster it comes down, and the more difficult it is to smash. Furthermore, the higher the ball goes, the more time you have to get into position. The defensive lob should be directed as deep in the opponent's court as possible, to make the putaway smash difficult. Stroke your high lobs down the middle of the court, to prevent errors caused by aiming too close to the sidelines.

After hitting your high defensive lob, you should move to a position about fifteen feet behind the center of the baseline to prepare to return the smash.

If after your opponent hits his overhead you are still in an undesirable court position, you can lob again. When the opponent is very close to the net as he smashes, it is often advisable to hit another lob. Try not to be forced to chase down too many smashes; although smashing requires considerable energy, so does running down distant overheads.

If you decide to return his smash as a normal groundstroke, it is usually best to hit at medium speed. Attempting to stroke a hard passing shot off a smash is very risky. When your opponent allows your deep defensive lobs to bounce, but lacks a good overhead, think about coming up to the net behind your lob.

MISCELLANEOUS REMARKS ON THE LOB

Difficulty of lobbing a low, short ball. There is one situation in which it is extremely difficult to execute an effective lob. This is when you are placed in a position to lob off a low and short ball. Getting your body weight behind and underneath your opponent's low angled volley is almost impossible, and accuracy is usually lacking. A few volleyers make extensive use of the angled volley to nullify lobbing attacks.

Lobs are easiest with wood and composition rackets. Like other touch shots, effective lobs are easier to produce with wood and the new composition rackets. Precise lobbing with a steel racket is tough, and aluminum is just fair for this purpose.

A classic in lob retrieving. Tenacious lobbers often get bruised in chasing down overhead smashes. It was not unusual to see Bobby Riggs come off the court with scrapes on his body from bumping against a fence. The Doherty brothers, who were exceptional lobbers during the turn of the century, surely kept the iodine handy.

Two of the most fantastic lobbing retrievers I have ever seen were the Ecuadorians Miguel Olivera and Eduardo Zuleta. Besides having excellent ball control and touch, they were blessed with unusual speed afoot. In singles play on slow clay courts they could drive some excellent smashers to drink. I have seen them force opponents to hit as many as sixty smashes in a match. By consistently returning each smash with a lob, the two South Americans would force their rivals to attempt more powerful smashes. Eventually they would extract an error. Olivera and Zuleta reached what was probably their lobbing pinnacle as a doubles team against two big smashers in a tournament in Tennessee. The hard smashing and fine lobbing had been going on for some time during this match. The more these two little "human flies" would lob, the harder the smashes would come back. Toward the end of a particularly lengthy point, overheads were being hit with so much zeal and force they sounded like thunder claps. By this time Olivera and Zuleta were perched with their backs to the fence. Suddenly, a smash was made with such power that the ball, after bouncing inside the court, bounded over the fence. The spectators started to applaud and the smashers breathed a sigh of relief. But the point was not over! Olivera had run out through the gate and returned the ball from behind the fence! He came back on the court and the point continued until finally a smash was hit and missed in desperation.

Although net men are usually in a position to apply pressure, great lobbers on slow courts can occasionally give a competent smasher the feeling that he has no overhead at all.

So far we have been concerned with groundstroke strategies. The ball you have been dealing with has hit the ground before your having returned it to the opponent. Although you can be offensive from the baseline area, this can be somewhat difficult. In the next four chapters we will discuss offensive strokes and tactics, including serving, volleying, and smashing. Top players are sound in these departments, as points can be taken from an opponent very efficiently and promptly with these strokes.

Chapter **13**

TACTICS WHILE PLAYING AT THE NET

Coming to the net ends points quickly, one way or the other. Points come to a dramatic ending. There are good reasons for you not to remain always in the back of your court.

WHY COME TO THE NET?

First, you should come to the net if you are capable of winning points in this area, and if you lose most of the points when you remain in the back of the court. Second, when your opponent is fearful of your winning a high percentage of points by coming to the net, you force him to hit deeper, harder, riskier balls. In addition, when you do come to the net, opponents tend to take their eyes off the ball. They will often start watching you instead of the ball. And, by standing at the net, you put pressure on your opponent by restricting his target area. He can no longer hit safely down the middle of the court, and high above the net. Finally, when you are at the net, your opponent is forced to take the ball earlier and hit harder than if you are in the back of the court.

APPLYING CONSTANT PRESSURE AT THE NET

For some advanced players it can be an excellent tactical move practically to camp at the net. By moving to the forecourt on every second, third, or fourth ball, you prevent an opponent from acquiring a good stroking rhythm. A big advantage in applying constant pressure is the fact that you (the net man) develop precision on volleys and smashes, since you are hitting so many of them. If you approach infrequently, you can easily lose feel on your forecourt shots. About the only advantage of spacing trips to the net far apart is that you will have the element of surprise slightly in your favor.

PROPER NET POSITION

As a general policy, when taking a position in the forecourt, stand slightly toward the sideline nearest the baseliner as he is hitting the ball. If the opponent is standing at the center mark of his baseline, place yourself in the middle of your court.

Ordinarily, you should stand about ten feet from the net. The closer to the net you move, the better the angle for putting the ball away toward the sides of the court and the fewer the chances of your hitting the ball into the net. With some opponents it is difficult to maintain this close-to-the-net position, even if you are very quick. If your opponent has a good lob, you might have to do your split stop sixteen or eighteen feet from the net. In this deep position you also have more time to react to the ball. If your opponent seldom lobs, stand as close as six feet from the net. In this case you can use a slow approach shot to afford you the time to move closer to the barrier.

With more experience you will sense how close to the net you can venture. You can gain forecourt ability by engaging in volleying-and-smashing drills. In addition, you should play an occasional practice set by serving and rushing to the net behind the serve. Playing on hard courts encourages the use of the forecourt game, as does playing doubles. In doubles, on any surface, most players other than beginners are usually best off by taking the net. Incidentally, when playing the forecourt, it is best to use a racket that has a lighter-than-usual head.

RUSHING THE NET IN PRESSURE MATCHES

There is a feeling among some tournament players that in a pressurized showdown between an evenly matched net rusher and a baseliner, the volleyer will win. The rationale for this is that slightly more precision and control are necessary to pass or lob over an opponent than are required to volley and smash, and a volley is inherently the most devastating shot because of the angle that can be achieved from close up at the net and the speed of the ball.

In a Davis Cup match in Paris such a classic baseliner-versus-volleyer duel took place between Gordon Forbes, the attacking South African, and Gerard Pilet, whose passing shots were exemplary. According to their records, the two players were about equal, but Forbes clobbered the Frenchman by applying relentless net pressure during the match.

PHYSICAL TOLL ON NET RUSHER

It is generally true that the volleyer who positions himself close to the net expends more energy than the baseliner. About the only case in which the volleyer (who moves in tight on the net) will work less than his baseline opponent is when he angle volleys short toward the open court, and smashes toward any possible opening. If you go to the net only behind your own serve, you usually do not become physically exhausted. However, when you also come in when the opponent is serving, you will likely become very tired.

Regarding energy loss, there is a considerable difference between volleying within ten feet or so of the net and positioning yourself around the service line of the midcourt area. Although the former is physically demanding, the latter can be done with less effort than playing at the baseline.

If you do not have as much stamina as your opponent, use periodic advances to the net as a means of keeping yourself in the match physically. The following hypothetical situation is one that all of us might find ourselves in. You are involved in a tennis match on a slow, red-clay court, in the eastern or southern U.S., in July. Your opponent has about the same stroking ability as you do. The temperature is ninety-two degrees, and the humidity is ninety percent. You are sweating when you first walk on the court and are in only fair condition. The match starts and you discover your opponent is like a human backboard and is in top physical condition. He does not come to the net, and is working you hard by drop-shotting and lobbing. Under these rough, but not too unusual, conditions, unless you are in superb physical shape, you have about an hour and a half or less to beat this guy. If you cannot do it by then, you are probably down the tubes. This is the perfect situation in which to speed up play by coming to the net.

GETTING HIT BY THE BALL WHILE PLAYING THE NET

For those of you who might have some fear of coming to the net because of being hit by the ball, do not be overly concerned. You can easily overcome this apprehension by practicing close volleys across the net with a friend, or by standing within seven or eight feet of a backboard and volleying against it. Although I have read of a serious accident or two, I have never been on a court where someone has been permanently injured after being struck by a tennis ball. I have been hit in every conceivable place on my body, and am still fit enough to walk out on the court for more punishment.

Chapter **14**

VOLLEYING TACTICS

The volley is most effective on fast courts such as asphalt and grass. Although it can produce winning points on clay, a strong approach shot or serve is usually necessary to make the volley succeed. The volley is an offensive shot. Nevertheless, there are a few fine players who are in essence "pushers at the net" until they can obtain a high and easy volley to put away.

WHY DOES THE VOLLEYER HAVE TO REACT QUICKLY?

Quickness is essential for good volleying. A player has less time to prepare for the volley than he has for the groundstroke, for the following three reasons:

1. The ball hit by the groundstroker to the volleyer travels a shorter distance than a ball going from baseline to baseline. (When both players are at the middle of their baselines, having a backcourt exchange, they are seventy-eight feet apart. When the volleyer is standing on the center service line, ten feet from the net, and the opponent is hitting from the center mark at his baseline, they are only forty-nine feet apart. Often, the volleyer must react to a ball hit only twenty to thirty feet from him.)
2. When a ball hits the ground, it loses approximately fifty percent of its speed. A ball you volley, or hit "on the fly," is therefore going one hundred percent faster than one you allow to bounce.
3. The longer a ball travels through the air, the more speed it loses. (This occurs dramatically after the ball reaches its maximum height. Often, the volleyer has to react so quickly that the ball does not have time to slow down in flight before contact.)

WHO SHOULD CONCENTRATE ON PERFECTING VOLLEYS?

Although all good players must have a sound volley, there are some who should concentrate intensely on

perfecting it. Those who live in areas where there are almost exclusively hard courts, such as in California and Arizona, should practice the volley extensively. Also, those who have naturally powerful serves should work on the volley since their deliveries often enable them to come to the net. A tall and agile player with a powerful service has exceptional qualifications to become a menacing volleyer.

BRIEF VOLLEYING TIPS

When you go into the volley-ready position, your racket should be held higher than on the groundstroke. This is because the path of the racket swing for the volley is in a slightly high-to-low direction. As you await the ball near the net, you should bend your knees and spread your legs, to assume a lower position than you would on backcourt groundstrokes. When your knees are bent, your balance is good, and you can spring quickly to intercept the passing shot. If you stay low, your eyes will be closer to the level of the ball, and you will be better prepared to receive a ball coming only three and a half feet or so off the ground.

The volley stroke itself is quite simple, and is taught during the first lesson by some tennis teachers. The volley is a short stroke with practically no backswing. The shoulder turn alone will usually suffice for backswing power. When the stroke is short and undercut (sliced), there is potential to develop angle and drop volleys; these are difficult volleys when using long and flat strokes. You should hit the volley well in front of your body so that you can

1. gain stable body power
2. meet the ball closest to the net (where errors will be minimized)
3. return the ball to the baseliner as quickly as possible, so he will have less time to react.

Although beginning players should use very little wrist on any shot, tournament competitors usually use some wrist on the volley, to gain power. The volley should be made with a long step to gain maximum yet safe power through weight transference. On the forehand volley, the left foot meets the ground at the same time the racket meets the ball; on the backhand volley, the same applies, but for the right foot.

VOLLEY PATTERNS

The key element in a successful volley attack is to move very quickly to the net and to position yourself close to it. If, after serving, you can run from the baseline to the service line in a period of one second or less, you are moving well. One-point-two or -three seconds is not that bad, whereas nine tenths of a second is very good, and eight tenths is excellent. (When timing a person, start the stopwatch when you hear the racket hit the ball on the serve, and stop it when you see the player's body crossing on top of the service line.)

Naturally, the faster the player runs to the net, the quicker he meets the volley, and the easier and more accurate the volley becomes. If you arrive at the net quickly, you will rarely be passed cleanly on return of service. Those who have this ability, and who have a firm and accurate volley, can be treacherous opponents.

Age takes its toll on a volleyer. I have seen some quick, agile volleyers who were great as young men but became only average volleyers as they passed forty or forty-five years of age. It is difficult for older players to move quickly to the net over the haul of a long match. Nevertheless, your volley stroke itself, as well as your groundstrokes, can remain sound as you age. Good volleyers of any age know they should move close to the net and meet the ball before it falls below the level of the net.

Deep-first-volley strategy. Many fine servers are faced with such fast returns that they can barely advance to the service line before having to hit their first volley. The initial volley is treated like an approach shot, and aimed deep to one of the baseline corners or down the middle. After making the first volley, the volleyer should move close to the net where he will be in position to angle his second volley away for a winner. Most good volleyers attempt to block low balls back deep and to sock high balls away for winners. Although the deep-volley concept is reasonably effective on fast courts, it is vulnerable on slow courts because it can be countered with the lob as well as the passing shot.

Short volley aimed away from the baseliner. An alternative to the deep-volley tactic is to place volleys short and near the sidelines of the court. This strategy also involves hitting the volley to that particular sideline that will make the opponent run the farthest. For the obvious reason I call it the "punishing volley" (*Fig. 14.1*). If the opponent is in one corner or the other and aims his passing shot down the line, the "punishing-volleyer" will aim crosscourt and short. If the opponent aims his passing shot crosscourt, you should hit down the line and short (*Fig. 14.2*). This is the only volleying pattern that will force the baseliner to work harder than the net man. The true disciple of the punishing volley will never hit behind a baseliner to give the latter physical respite.

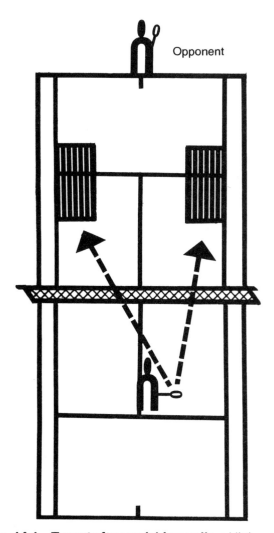

Fig. 14.1   Targets for punishing volley. Hitting short volleys nullifies the opponent's lob, and makes passing shots difficult.

79

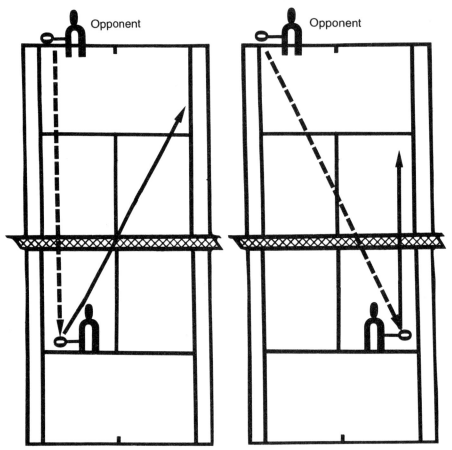

Fig. 14.2 Punishing-volley tactic is aiming toward the open court.
Fig. A   When opponent hits passing shot down the line, volley crosscourt.
B   When opponent hits passing shot crosscourt, volley down the line.

In order for this tactic to be successful, the short volleys must be kept low and firm. The lowness of the ball makes passing very difficult for the opponent, and it virtually nullifies his lob. For the latter reason this punishing-volley strategy is effective on the slowest of surfaces. Although this tactic is very predictable, it will do the baseliner very little good to know where the next shot is going.

There is another pair of targets that you can occasionally use. These targets are located close to the net and toward the middle of the service box (*Fig. 14.3*). If this volley is kept low, it can be an effective shot. There is safety, since you are not aiming close to the sidelines or to the net, as you would on a touch volley.

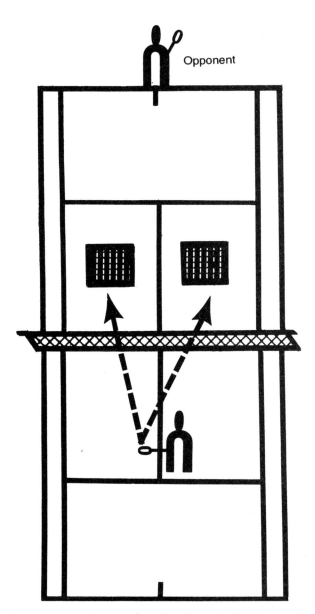

Fig. 14.3 Safe, short volley targets. This is an alternative for the inexperienced volleyer who cannot manage the punishing-volley tactic. The ball must be kept low.

Why do very few players use the short-angled-volley technique? Players develop a habit of deep volleying for several reasons. First, aspiring players have rarely seen a true exponent of the short angled volley, since there are very few in the world today. (Randall King, a ranking player in the eastern U.S., is very effective in utilizing this style of volley.) Second, most competitors do not practice this volley. When players work on volleys, one person usually positions himself behind the center of the baseline, and thus there is no angle-volleying. When tennis players practice close volleys, they do not angle-volley. Backboard or wall volleys are also hit straight, and not angled. Angled volleying is difficult to practice, since it is virtually impossible to sustain a rally unless you have three players. The most effective method of learning the punishing short angled volley, as well as reprogramming a deep volleyer, is with a ball machine. Lastly, if a player is incapable of taking a short backswing and undercutting the ball, the angled volley is extremely difficult.

The automatic volley. A second alternative to the deep volley, which is similar to the punishing volley, is the "automatic volley." In this volley pattern a player uses the same short sideline targets as in the punishing volley; however, he aims his volleys only crosscourt. It is called the automatic volley because both the forehand and backhand are hit crosscourt and short. The advantage of the automatic volley is that you learn the two shots extremely well by hitting constantly toward the same targets. Most players aim toward any one of five or six volley targets on a court.

A practitioner of this volley was Budge Patty, a handsome American who resided and played in Europe for most of his tennis career. Patty was an incredible net rusher who used the automatic volley exclusively on the forehand side. I had heard about Patty's forehand volley for years, but unfortunately he rarely came to the U.S. to show his skills. I finally had the opportunity to see him in the championship match of the City of Miami tournament, against Gardnar Mulloy. Patty's forehand volley was even better than I had imagined; he made winner after winner with this shot. If he did not make an outright placement, Patty would extract a feeble return and then produce the winning volley. Mulloy knew very well beforehand the direction of Patty's forehand volley, but it did not do him any good, since the volley was so devastating. When victorious, Patty would often come to the net and stand a few feet on the backhand side of his forecourt, inviting a forehand volley that he would always angle short and cross court.

Volleying high floaters from the backcourt. Another volleying tactic used by tournament players on clay courts is to take a backcourt-ready position on, or slightly inside, the baseline, and to volley and come to the net on any ball that floats up high. (Volleyers rarely get the opportunity to use this tactic on cement, since good players seldom float high balls or hit loops on this surface.) Players who use this pattern serve and come in just a step or two, and then wait to see if their opponent returns their service high, slow, and safe. If such a return is made, they volley the ball and come to the net.

ANTICIPATING YOUR OPPONENT'S RETURN WHILE VOLLEYING

Anticipating passing shots. A volleyer has a distinct advantage if he can determine beforehand where his opponent is going to hit the ball. On ordinary passing shots, most good players will mix it up, hitting some balls toward one side and some toward the other. For example, they will hit sixty percent of backhand passing shots down the line and forty percent crosscourt, or vice versa. You, the volleyer, cannot take full advantage of this kind of six-to-four ratio; however, when you notice a two-to-one pattern, you can anticipate to your advantage.

Good anticipation is also achieved by watching the ball contact the strings of your opponent's racket. When you do this, you are able to gain better timing of his shot. You become a split second faster in reaching the opponent's shot. Also, watch how the opponent sets his body, especially if you are in a vulnerable position at the net. The way he lines up his feet and then transfers or does not transfer his weight forward can offer clues ragarding direction and power.

There are specific signs that indicate whether an opponent is going to hit a crosscourt or a down-the-line passing shot (*Fig. 14.4*). Usually, the elbow is farther out on the crosscourt passing shot than on the down-the-line shot. Watch for the telltale clue of the dropped racket head for the lob. Reading an opponent is difficult when his arm-and-racket action is very fast.

Fig. 14.4 Anticipating the direction of the opponent's forehand passing shot.
A   Clues indicating a forehand crosscourt passing shot. Feet are in square-stance position and widely spread. The right shoulder is dropped, and the left shoulder is raised.

B Clues indicating a forehand down-the-line passing shot. Feet are in square-stance position and close together. The left shoulder is dropped, and the right shoulder is raised.

An effective passing-shot-anticipation tactic, and one that can be combined with observing the baseliner's footwork and body position, is first to cover the crosscourt passing shot; then, if your opponent does not aim crosscourt, you move to cut off the down-the-line passing shot. You can also do the reverse, and key on the down-the-line shot first and then move crosscourt. When caught in a defensive position, some volleyers choose to block off all down-the-line shots and give their opponents the sharply angled crosscourt winner (*Fig. 14.5*).

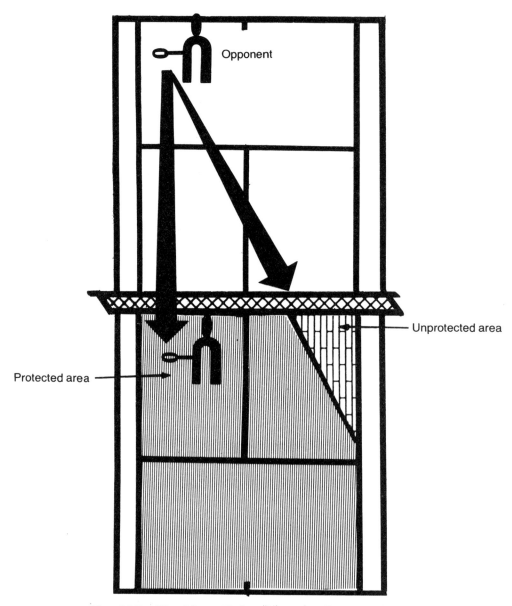

Opponent

Unprotected area

Protected area

Fig. 14.5 Blocking off the down-the-line passing shot and allowing the sharply angled crosscourt opening.

Whenever you are moved far out of position at the net because of an opponent's sideline shot, be sure to be quick to recover proper position immediately after making your return. In the majority of cases your opponent will hit his next shot toward the open court.

A fine Austrian international-class tennis player, Freddie Huber, used a slightly different method of intercepting an opponent's passing shots. Huber, a redhead, had been a hockey goalie, and he simply transferred his skills from the ice rink to the tennis forecourt. Just as an opponent thought he had hit a clean passing shot by him, Huber would not just reach wide to block it back but would *dive* out to cut off the ball! Although he covered the net like two men, Huber paid a penalty for his zealous net guardianship. He probably has the unfortunate distinction of having suffered more cuts and bruises than any tennis player in history.

Anticipating return of service. Predicting the direction of a return of service is easier than guessing someone's passing-shot direction. If you have a very accurate and deep service, you will find that you can usually predict the direction of the return. I know strong-serving net rushers who take full advantage of an opponent's propensity not to vary return-of-service direction when faced with a deep and tough serve.

The stimulus of a big serve hit to one corner or the other will usually elicit the identical response over and over. Of course, some returns of service are so penetrating that knowing their direction beforehand is of no great consequence.

Drawing shots by positioning. Earlier, I mentioned that Budge Patty used to entice players to hit to his great forehand volley by positioning himself on his backhand side. He knew that players were vulnerable to this tactic because they tended to hit toward the open part of the court. In addition to using this positioning tactic to draw an opponent's passing shot into your strength, you can occasionally use it to extricate yourself from a difficult situation. For example, if you made a weak volley and found yourself in bad forecourt position with your opponent on his service line ready to crunch the soft ball, you could do the following: move near one sideline, and wait there as the opponent takes his groundstroke backswing; just as he is starting his forward swing, take a couple of steps across and close up the opening (*Fig. 14.6*). By employing this tactic, and completely blocking off one side of the court, you will often find yourself winning the point when otherwise you would have barely stood a chance.

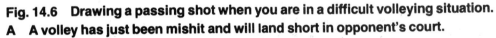

Fig. 14.6   Drawing a passing shot when you are in a difficult volleying situation.
A   A volley has just been mishit and will land short in opponent's court.

Fig. 14.6B Step quickly to one side of the court and invite opponent to hit to the obvious opening.

Fig. 14.6C   If opponent hits toward opening, you will likely have a winning volley.

Drop volley. The touch, stop, or drop volley should be used when you are within six feet of the net and are faced with a ball below the level of the top of the net (*Fig. 14.7*). (A high, short ball should not be drop-volleyed when it can easily be put away.) It is important that your body weight be going forward on the drop volley so that your opponent cannot "read" your intentions.

Fig. 14.7 Drop volley when you are very close to the net and the ball is too low to be volleyed away for a winner.

Lob volley. This shot is used when both you and your opponent are at the net and you are being forced to hit up from a very low volleying position (*Fig. 14.8*). You should try to lob-volley the ball over his head.

Fig. 14.8 Lob volley when the opponent is very close to the net and you are trapped in a low defensive position in the forecourt.

Half volley. Actually, this is not a member of the volley family but is a groundstroke taken as a quick pickup. It is usually hit from the midcourt area as a player is attempting to move up close to the net. Be sure to use a short backswing, and very little pace, since the ball is being struck low to the ground, and very close to the net. Try to place the half volley deep, so that you can gain good net position. Sometimes it is advisable to hit your half volley short and barely over the net, but this requires excellent touch. While in the back of your court, you might find the half volley a valuable shot when your opponent hits a scorching drive that bounces within a foot or two of your baseline and you do not have the time to retreat and take it as a waist-high ball.

Excepting Pancho Segura, whose weak serve often forced him to half volley, the greatest exponent of no-man's-land play (hitting balls on the rise), and its attendant half volleys, was Henri Cochet. In recognition of his outstanding ability, the Frenchman was elected to the International Tennis Hall of Fame in 1976 with the other "Musketeers," J.-René Lacoste, Jean Borotra, and Jacques Brugnon.

When your opponent is forced to half volley, you should often be on your way to the net. Unless he is extremely gifted, he will likely be hitting upward, in a defensive manner.

Even if you have the greatest half volley and volley in the world, you have to possess one more weapon to be successful while playing the net. A net rusher will be lobbed unmercifully if he does not have a formidable overhead smash—our next topic of discussion.

Chapter 15

SMASHING TACTICS

A good smash is an essential element of a successful net attack. Without it, any net offensive can be thwarted. On fast surfaces, many players have overhead smashes that can adequately put away the lob. On clay courts the act of banging away a lob for a winner is a much more difficult proposition. Great power and accuracy are necessary for slower courts, and very few players have this consistent capability.

Mervyn Rose possessed a tremendous overhead. Although he was a net rusher, Rose, interestingly, wreaked havoc on clay courts. His smash was so automatic on the slowest of surfaces that players were forced to hit to his volley. Since Rose's volley was almost as devastating as his overhead, his opponents were left with an unenviable choice when he was at the net.

WHERE SHOULD YOU AIM YOUR SMASH?

The more power you use, the farther from the lines you can place your overhead and still put the ball away. Try to remember to use only enough power to perform the task at hand. Do not smash a ball at 100 mph if a 70-mph shot will suffice. Beginners should simply aim for either the backhand or forehand side of the court, whereas advanced players who lack overwhelming power should aim four feet or so from one of the sidelines, provided they are not caught too deep in their court. When your smash hits four feet from the opponent's sideline at his service line, you will have an excellently angled overhead. When your smash lands four feet from the opponent's sideline near his baseline, you will likely have a winner, or at least extract a weak lob in return (*Fig. 15.1*).

As a general rule, when standing inside the service line, try for a clean winner by using maximum power with placement. When smashing from a position between your service line and baseline, be content to place the ball to his backhand with medium force. In this case, do not aim too close to the lines, as it is not worth the risk. Naturally, when your opponent is out of

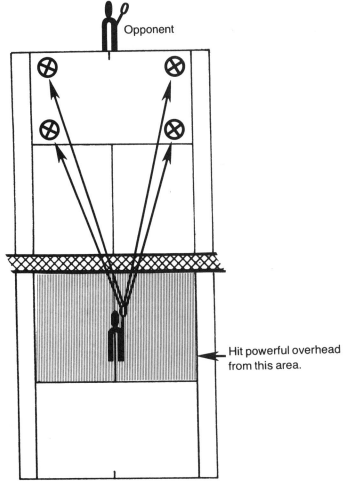

Fig. 15.1 Overhead-smash targets for tournament players. When you have good balance in the forecourt, hit with power and aim four or five feet from the singles sideline.

position, you should direct your overhead toward the open court.

Unless you can put the overhead away cleanly, place it to the opponent's backhand side. This is especially true when standing on your own forehand side. Because of the flexibility of an opponent's forehand groundstroke, you can occasionally be passed as he drives back your overhead. When smashing to the opponent's backhand, you can almost be guaranteed the opportunity to make an additional play on the ball, assuming the opponent returns it.

ANTICIPATING THE LOB

If your opponent has an inclination to use the offensive lob, pay particular attention to his backswing and body positioning as he prepares to stroke the ball. The two giveaway signs of the lob are the lowering of the racket head (good players do this only at the last second) and the leaning of the body weight away from the net (tournament players never do this on an offensive lob) (*Fig. 15.2*).

Drilling is an excellent method of developing anticipation of the lob; the baseliner should mix unannounced lobs with low passing shots to the volleyer. Of course, drilling is also the most effective means of developing the smash.

WHEN TO ALLOW THE LOB TO BOUNCE

Try not to permit low and medium-high lobs to bounce, as this allows an opponent too much time to regain good court position. Also, when a lob is allowed to bounce, the opportunity for a clean putaway is diminished because the opponent has ample time to take excellent court position, and you will likely be smashing from the back part of your court.

When the opponent's lob is hit very high, and the wind is not blowing against you, it is advisable to allow the lob to bounce. An extremely high lob is difficult to time; therefore, the possibilities of an error are reduced by letting it bounce. Deep lobs that are taken after the first bounce should be hit with a slight amount of spin, whereas those taken on the fly are best hit flat.

ADDITIONAL TIPS ON THE SMASH

Take as many lobs with the forehand overhead as possible. The backhand overhead should be brought into play only when you absolutely cannot execute the forehand smash. Such an instance is when an opponent hits a quick offensive lob toward your backhand side. Among the few players who can put a backhand smash away are Californians Stan Smith and Dave Reed. Gene Scott, a top Eastern player, could also clobber this difficult shot.

Fig. 15.2 Two giveaway signs of the lob. 1. The racket head is dropped; and 2. opponent's weight is on the back foot. When you see either of these telltale clues, move quickly from the net.

When you hit the smash, do not take a full backswing, by bringing the racket down by your knees, as you would on a serve. Wait for the ball with the racket pointing straight up in the air, and then simply drop your racket head behind your back and swing up and forward. The fine timing required on the overhead is too difficult to master with a full backswing.

Although the backswing on the serve and the smash differ, the rudiments of the two strokes are the same (racket drop behind the back, and forward swing). Because of the similarity of the strokes, you will discover that practicing the serve will improve your overhead smash. The smasher who uses an abbreviated (hammer-nail) service action, in which the racket is simply brought over the shoulder and behind the back, and who employs the same grip for service and overhead, has a slight advantage.

Here are two additional tips. Successful smashing depends on carefully watching the lob as it descends. You must keep as close an eye on the ball during an overhead smash as you do at any time while hitting a tennis ball. And, the smash is doubly difficult to execute in the wind, so do not expect to have good timing under these conditions, and certainly slow down your swing.

The smash is an offensive weapon that a good player must master, but is not usually brought into play on every point. There is another, more frequently used shot that is similar in execution to the overhead smash but is much more crucial, as it determines the result of a large number of points. It is the serve.

Chapter **16**

SERVING TACTICS

In men's-tournament tennis, the serve, more than any other stroke, determines a player's potential. A big service is absolutely necessary to win on fast courts, and it helps a player win on slow surfaces as well. You have a decided advantage in developing a fine service if you have a good throwing arm. A long baseball or javelin toss is indicative of good serving potential. If you have a strong throwing arm, you should learn the proper service action and practice serving as much as possible in order to exploit your natural talent.

OBJECTIVES OF A GOOD SERVER

The beginning player is usually at a disadvantage when he serves, because he is prone to double-fault. On the other hand, the tournament player will usually win the majority of games he serves, assuming his opponent is on his same level. A good player hopes to extract an error on the service return, or score an ace, during each serving game on even the slowest of surfaces. On grass, most good servers are usually seeking two errors, or hoping for about two aces, in each game. If you are unable to force an error during your serving games, then you should at least be able to extract a short ball or two that you are able to attack.

Holding your own service. As an advanced player, you should view the holding of service as the criterion for determining a change in serving tactics. If you are winning all of your service games, continue your normal service pattern. If your service is broken once, think about changing tactics. If you lose service twice in a row, definitely make a tactical change.

Your tactical options include serving to various targets with different speeds and spins, serving high balls and low balls, serving and coming to net, staying back on service, and serving and then taking two steps in and stopping.

FIRST-SERVICE TACTICS

Try to get more than fifty percent of first serves into play. Achieving a high percentage of good first serves minimizes your opponent's opportunity to take full advantage of your weaker second serve. A smart opponent knows that you will not hit bullets or hit too close to the lines on your second service, for fear of double-faulting. Therefore, the opponent will stand in closer to the net when receiving your second serve, and can often mistreat it with a powerful return. An additional reward for getting a high percentage of first serves into play is that you save energy by hitting one instead of two serves during a given point. Stretched over the length of a match, this can preserve your stamina.

Achieving a better-than-fifty-percent average on first serves should not be the criterion for all players. If your adversary is returning all of your medium-speed first serves, but is missing one in four of those hit with more pace, you will likely profit by bludgeoning the first service, even if you put a lower percentage in play.

Get the first serve in play on important points. On crucial points, you should almost certainly serve at three-quarter speed, to avoid the pressure of having to make a good second serve. All advanced players should develop the ability to put eighty percent or more of medium-speed serves into play when the need arises.

On slow courts, when you are not forcing errors or short balls with your first service, you should slow it down, to reduce exertion. This wasted energy can be put to better use on your other strokes. There have been many international-class clay-court specialists who simply put the serve in play to start the point.

SECOND-SERVICE TACTICS

Avoid double-faulting at any time during an important match. Since you should be striving to increase second-service power during unimportant practice matches, you should expect double faults during these sessions. The point here is that you should learn beforehand what your limits of power and accuracy are on second service without having to experiment at crucial moments.

There are some occasions when a few double faults are permissible. For example, Barry MacKay, a big, powerful U.S. Davis Cup player from Ohio, served a large number of double faults in his matches a number of years ago. In hitting bombs on his second service on fast courts, MacKay took a calculated risk, knowing that he would miss approximately twenty percent of his second serves. However, he also knew that when he did get his second serve in play, there was the likelihood of extracting an error or a defensive return, and even of his serving an outright winner. MacKay did not have the ability to hit an accurate overspinning second serve, so rather than throw in a marshmallow, he went for broke. But MacKay's tactics are strictly a stopgap measure for the big server on extremely fast courts.

SERVICE PLACEMENT

Should you constantly hammer at a weakness, or just exploit it on important points? As an alert player, you should quickly make comparisons between an opponent's backhand and forehand return of service. Usually, one is stronger than the other. The question then becomes, Should you attack the weakness at every opportunity, or just on important points?

There are a few tennis authorities who contend that when we constantly pursue an opponent's stroking weakness, it will strengthen during the match. In my opinion, there is an equally valid argument that the weakness will become *weaker* as the match progresses. Although stroking consistency can be honed within a given match, actual development requires weeks and months of practice. It is a rare case when a true weakness turns into strength during a two-hour period of a match.

One of the most important consequences of unrelenting pounding at a vulnerable spot is that you make your opponent aware of his weakness and, in turn, undermine his confidence (*Fig. 16.1*). Thus, it is usually best to aim the vast majority of shots to the obvious weakness, and vary the direction only once in awhile so that he will have some doubt as to the placement of your serve.

Fig. 16.1 Constantly playing opponent's weaknesses can shake his confidence. Do not conceal your intentions.

The forehand versus the backhand return of service. On the beginning level, the backhand return of service is almost always the weakest stroke, and should be exploited. On the tournament level, the backhand is usually the steadiest return with the least power. Many service receivers will be content to slice the backhand return with medium speed, but will hit hard forehand returns. Many opponents can hurt us by clobbering a slow or medium-speed serve with the forehand.

However, many players do not have the flexibility to block back a hard service softly with a forehand. They tend to make errors when attempting, with a full backswing, to return powerful and deep services placed to their forehands. Therefore, I prefer to serve extremely hard to the forehand side, and serve medium-speed and slow balls to the backhand.

The eight service targets. Fine service placement is difficult because of the mechanics of the serve itself. When a player hits *up* on a service (for overspin), with terrific speed, it is very hard to attain accuracy. Incidentally, slow servers do not have to use as much spin as hard servers, as gravity plays a more important role in bringing the ball into the service box. Slow servers can console themselves knowing they have greater accuracy potential then their hard-serving counterparts, and can expend less energy.

While giving Frank Hammond, the dean of service-line judges, a ride from Forest Hills to Manhattan one day, I asked him to tell me the name of the server whose deliveries landed deeper in the opponent's service box than any other. Was it the crunching serve of Arthur Ashe or of John Newcombe? No, it was Ken Rosewall's slow-to-medium-speed service that often landed on the back edge of the opponent's service line. Frank said that calling Rosewall's serves put him to the ultimate test.

Very few tournament players are able to hit a one-square-yard target, deep in the opponent's serving box (fifty-seven feet away), even eight times out of ten. In addition to hitting the serve with a glancing blow, the big server must generate power with the stomach, shoulder, leg, and wrist. It is indeed a highly coordinated effort. Also, the good server must almost catapult himself from the baseline toward the service line immediately after serving.

In *Figure 16.2*, eight serving targets are depicted. As you become more experienced, you will find depth and consistency will improve.

Use variety in placement and spin. Just as a baseball pitcher, a boxer, or a football quarterback varies

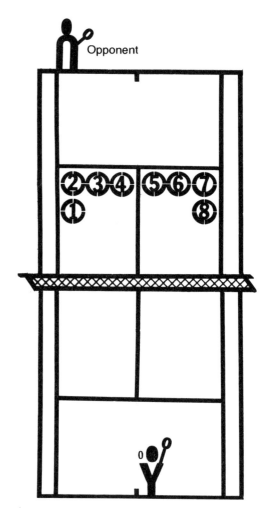

Fig. 16.2 Eight service targets.
1.   Serve slice here.
2.   On big points, do not serve here and follow to net.
3. & 6.   Jam opponent by serving here to reduce the angle of his return.
4.   Serve most of deuce-court serves here.
5.   Serve very deep here if you plan to rush the net.
7.   Serve most of ad-court serves here
8.   Serve twist here, especially if receiver cannot underspin the return of service; also, take a step in and be ready to volley a soft return of the twist.

his attack, so should the tennis server. When an adversary knows what to expect, he can gear himself mentally for the defense. The smart server keeps the receiver guessing by being unpredictable.

Try to hit all spin serves with good pace. When a slice or an American twist comes in with speed, it is doubly effective, because the receiver has less time to react to the spin. If you cannot hit your serve with gusto, but have a good volley and like to rush the net, try to develop a slice service. Since the slice stays low and forces the receiver to hit up, the volleyer often receives balls that can be dealt with easily.

When a receiver is standing two or three feet behind his baseline, use the American-twist service if you have one in your repertoire. Since the twist is a slow serve, the server has extra time to move closer to the net than with other serves. When the opponent returns the twist from behind his baseline, it allows the server ample time to move very close to the net. A number of years ago I regularly played a nationally ranked slugger who belted all balls extremely hard. He took my twists well behind his baseline, and pounded them as hard as possible. I would easily intercept his returns and make winning volleys. If he had returned from *inside* the baseline, I would have had no chance with this pattern of play. You might ask, What is the most effective method of forcing the opponent behind the baseline, where he will be vulnerable to the twist? It is to serve a hard and deep ball that will force him to err if he stands on or inside the baseline.

SPEED OF SERVICE

Racket-head speed is essential to effective serving. Try to swing your racket at about the same speed on first and second serves. (You will simply have more spin on the second serve than on the first.) By using the same amount of racket-head speed on both serves you will attain better rhythm for your second serve, and will probably commit fewer double faults.

SERVING AND FOLLOWING THE SERVE TO THE NET

Those with big enough serves to extract at least a waist- or thigh-high ball to volley can follow their serves to the net with some surety. If you are consistently given a service return at your shoetops, or forced to half volley, your serve is not strong enough to follow to the net. In this case you should attempt to

come to the net on your first groundstroke, providing the return of service is not too deep.

You have other options in regard to the serve-and-volley strategy. Occasionally you will come across an opponent who has, for example, a very strong return of service from the ad court, a weaker one from deuce, or vice versa. In this case you can rush the net after serving to the particular service box where you anticipate a weak return, then serve and stay back when going against his stronger return. Another possible reason for you to serve and come to the net only on one side is that you may be able to serve better into one service box than the other.

On clay courts, if you can hold service regularly by consistent and powerful serving, you have the advantage, since most players do not have this capability. Adriano Panatta, the six-foot-two-inch Italian, won both the French and Italian Championships in 1976 by consistently holding service in these clay-court events.

If you are planning to serve and volley, be sure to serve from within three or four feet of the center mark. By doing this you will be closer to the proper volleying position. Incidentally, if you have a weak second serve that players attack and follow to the net, try standing wide and serving wide to both the ad and deuce courts, so that your opponent's angled approaches to the net will be more difficult. Be careful of this play, since it can backfire if your opponent can slip the return down the line and come in behind it.

STANDING WIDE TO SERVE

Once in a while you will see a good server in singles who stands between the center mark and the singles sideline. Usually he will not rush net from this position. Bob Potthast, a former University of Iowa football player and a big server, did this successfully. When he put his huge bomb wide to either the deuce or the ad court, many opponents responded with an error because they were not used to a ball coming at them from such an angle in singles play.

USING THE UNDERHAND SERVICE

If you are a beginning player and cannot control your second service, you can serve underhand in order to minimize double faults. You might also serve underhand if your shoulder is hurting, in order to allow it rest. Bob Howe, a fine Australian doubles and mixed-doubles player, was once in this predicament and used this serve to help him get to the finals of the U.S. Doubles championship. A few advanced players will periodically use a spinning underhand service in order to break the rhythm of an opponent. When serving underhand with spin, it is often best to move to the net, since you can usually volley the return for a winner, providing you can get your racket on the return. Players who have very weak serves should contemplate using this service. An Indiana banker, Homer Shoop, served nothing but underhand serves, and was very effective. Many senior-tournament players he faced became exasperated trying to run down his spinning serves.

A knowledge of serving tactics is important in the education of a tennis player. Serving and stroking tactics are closely connected to the kind of court surface we play on, and the type of ball used. In the next two chapters we will deal with tactical variables that have little to do with the opponent but that are important to understand in order to play well.

Chapter 17

TACTICS FOR DIFFERENT SURFACES AND BALLS

STRATEGY AND ITS RELATIONSHIP TO COURT SURFACES

Experienced players are aware that tennis-court surfaces can differ markedly in their playability. One surface will differ from another in speed of the ball bounce, height of the ball bounce, and foot traction. Certain strokes and spins will react extremely well on some surfaces, yet will be very ineffective on others. One of the most vital aspects of a change in surfaces is the player's mental attitude. He must be prepared to switch from an offensive frame of mind to one of patience and defense, or vice versa. A player raised on European clay would be handicapped if he were forced to compete on a fast cement court in San Francisco. If the situation were reversed, and the Californian played on a clay court in Oviedo, Spain, or Antwerp, Belgium, he would be at a severe disadvantage until he learned the intricacies of the surface.

Great players such as Rod Laver, Don Budge, and Pancho Gonzales could win on all surfaces. Touring pros, who are regularly forced to change surfaces, acclimate themselves to new conditions within a few hours. Tennis players are fortunate when they receive exposure to both clay and hard courts while developing their games. A few players in the Northeastern part of the U.S. are able to make rapid surface switches, since they regularly experience play on clay, hard courts, artificial courts, grass, and wood (these last two surfaces are rapidly becoming extinct). As a result they have a good understanding of the game.

Following is a list of the important characteristics of and recommendations for each of the three major surfaces:

Hard Courts

1. Be very concerned about holding service.
2. Use less spin and more pace, since the surface increases ball speed.
3. Forget about using loops against almost any backcourt opponent who is a good volleyer.
4. Except to lob, do not move farther than three feet behind the baseline. From far behind the baseline, you can be attacked too easily. Occasionally, when in this position, you will be forced to half-volley. However, do not fear this shot on hard courts, since the ball bounce is relatively true. If you are a tournament-level player and you position yourself on the baseline, you can cut off high, deep shots before they have a chance to drive you far behind the baseline.
5. Hardly ever drop-shot an opponent who has an adequate volley. However, the drop *volley* can be effective.
6. A long backswing on groundstrokes is less important on hard courts, since the surface generates power. Often you will not have sufficient time to take the big backswing.
7. Approach shots do not have to be as precise as on clay courts. Sometimes a low and short ball near the sidelines will suffice as an approach to the net. A few players are effective in making approach shots from as deep as three feet behind their baseline.
8. Serving and rushing the net is not necessarily the most effective style of play except among high-ranking tournament players. Powerful serving, however, is very important.
9. Volleying is more effective than it is on clay because the footing is better and the courts are faster.

Clay Courts

1. Good physical conditioning is vital on slow clay and dirt courts. Since the ball is moving slower and is easier to retrieve and control than on other surfaces, rallies last longer. The ball can be

stroked nearer lines and corners, and the fatiguing drop shot can be put into play. Lengthen points if you are in better shape than your opponent; shorten them if you are not.

2. Deep and accurate groundstrokes are essential for a tough clay-court game. Steadiness is of great importance, so do not make unforced errors.

3. Green (quick-drying) clay courts play fast enough that a serve-and-volley game can be effective. On brown or red clay, it is more difficult to establish an attacking game.

4. Do not blast a ball unless you have worked yourself into an offensive position in which two shots can end the point.

5. You need to watch the ball more carefully than on hard surfaces because of the greater frequency of bad bounces.

6. Since clay courts can be slippery, it is advisable to wear a deck-type sneaker with deep grooves in the soles for traction.

7. Hitting high balls can be a very effective tactic because your opponent might have trouble getting leverage and a solid hit. High overspin loops and American-twist serves can be particularly troublesome for the opponent.

8. If possible, use the drop shot to bring a steady backcourt player out of his area of strength.

9. In order to play clay courts well you must know how to slide. A California hard-courter going to the South or to Europe must plan on spending a minimum of two or three months learning the intricacies of clay, including the slide.

10. The clay-court net game is not as effective as on other surfaces, because your backcourt opponent has too much time to run down your volleys. Also, since footing at the net is not as solid as it is on hard courts, the firm volley is more difficult. Right after a rain, or in high humidity, when the balls become heavy and slow, a net attack can be surprisingly successful. A backcourter might not be able to pass you.

11. On slippery clay courts, hitting behind your opponent ("wrong-footing" him) can be very effective, as changing direction is difficult.

12. On clay, unlike on hard courts, a player has innumerable tactical options. If one kind of strategy does not work, another can be used. Experience and proper use of strategy are usually part of a winning clay-court game.

Though I have included grass as a major surface, it is on its way out in tournament play in the United States. One of the reasons for this is that grass is impractical to maintain, and there are very few lawn courts in the country where a player can gain experience. (Wood is also a dying surface, since there are far superior indoor surfaces now available.)

Grass Courts

1. Serve and come to the net if you have even a mediocre volley. Since the bounces are low, and often unpredictable, the ball should be taken before hitting the ground whenever possible.

2. Speed of service (as well as of other shots) is of supreme importance, since the ball often skids on grass. Holding service is absolutely essential, as it is difficult to break serve on this surface.

3. Bending the legs and taking a low stroking position is imperative. An inflexible player is under a severe handicap on grass.

BALL DIFFERENCES

There are marked differences among the types of tennis ball used throughout the world for tournament play. For example, an American ball plays much faster than an Italian Pirelli. Some tournaments use pressure-less balls, which are slightly more jarring on the arm than those that are pressure-packed but which can retain their consistent bounce even after many sets of tennis.

After you open a can or box of balls, be very observant of their playing characteristics. Seasoned competitors know how different makes of balls play because of past experiences with them. American-made balls, if dropped from head height in room temperatures, should bounce to waist height.

The same can or box of balls will change in playability during a given match. New balls play faster than those used for a few games, and, as a result, you should play slightly more aggressively early in a match, or right after the ball change. Dirt or moisture from the ground (or from your hand) slows down balls, as does a fluffed-up cover. Some big hitters thrive in clay-court matches after balls become heavy, since the balls have less of a tendency to float out of court.

Soft or less lively balls react similarly to heavy balls and play slowly. European balls tend to play slower than American balls; thus, offensive weapons are not as important in Rome or Paris as they are in Los Angeles. Defensive specialists usually prefer slow balls, as well as slow courts; however, there are some who prefer hard and fast balls since they know their hard-hitting opponent will be more susceptible to errors. Drop shots and lobs can be hit accurately with softer balls, because the ball flattens out and stays longer on the racket strings. Slow European balls and courts encourage big backswings on strokes.

If the ball is hard and plays fast, you must be careful not to overhit. On cement, balls become lighter as a match progresses, but they still are not as fast as when they first come out of the can. As they do become lighter, you have to be particularly careful about hitting your lobs over the opponent's baseline.

If you are a tournament player, it is best to practice with the same brand or type of ball you will be using in your next match. If this is not practical, try to use balls that are as fast or faster than those to be used in the tournament. Adjusting from fast to slow balls and courts is usually easier than going from slow to fast conditions. In any case, it is unwise to practice with dead balls, since they are too easily controlled. Save dead balls for practice on a backboard.

In this chapter we have discussed the differences in court surfaces and balls. Another factor we must consider, since it is constantly changing, is the weather. Adjusting to changes in wind conditions, sunlight, and temperature is essential if one is to be an expert tactician.

Chapter 18

TACTICS IN DIFFERENT WEATHER CONDITIONS

Weather conditions are variables that a player must learn to adapt to. Tournament-tennis competitors know from experience the types of strokes and strategies that will and will not work in wind, poor light, heat, and cold. Such adverse conditions are frustrating, but the individual who becomes least distracted, and who utilizes proper tactics, can actually benefit from these conditions.

PLAYING IN THE WIND

Wind is a problem throughout the world. A good tennis player must learn to cope with winds, as they are a constant threat to good tennis at most of the world's outdoor courts. Winds of eight or ten miles per hour or more cause errors, and shorter, less satisfying rallies.

Strong wind tends to be an equalizer, and upsets become more prevalent. At a recent NCAA tennis championship in Corpus Christi, Texas, most seeded players fell early because of winds of twenty to thirty miles per hour. With the absence of big mountains, parts of Texas and certain Midwestern states have windy conditions. I have played tournaments in the South of France, with its mistral winds, and in Florida at which there were gusts of forty miles per hour. The result is that players from all these regions learn, of necessity, how to play the wind. Some South African coastal areas are "wind tunnels," and produce the best "wind players" in the world. Conversely, those who play most of their tennis indoors are hopeless in variable winds.

When you have scheduled a practice match and it turns out to be an extremely windy day, do not cancel your tennis, as many players do, but use this as an educational experience. Do not become irritated and discouraged if you are behind in score, since you can win games (and lose them) quickly under these conditions.

Becoming aware of wind direction. Develop a sensitivity in detecting the presence and direction of the wind. You will know the path of a strong downwind or crosswind the moment you walk on the court. As you warm up in these conditions, you can observe wind direction. Often, the wind pattern remains somewhat the same during the match. Once in a while, however, there will be a swirling or fluctuating wind. Sometimes it will blow in one direction, then, a moment later, reverse its course. There are other times when the wind will howl for a few minutes, and then suddenly quiet down.

You can sense the direction of the wind as it blows against your skin. Just before the start of a point, glance at the ground, or observe the movement of leaves or dirt. As you change sides, notice whether the net is blowing toward one side or the other. Also, if a bush or flag is nearby, notice the direction in which it is being blown.

Three specific suggestions to improve your play in any kind of wind. The suggestions can be applied to winds blowing with or against you.

1. When playing in the wind you must watch the ball more carefully because of sudden changes in the speed and direction of the ball.
2. Try not to commit yourself too quickly by taking a long backswing on a groundstroke.
3. When serving, lower your toss.
4. If there is a sudden gust of wind, it is advisable to wait a few seconds for it to die down before serving. Do not delay too long, though, since it can be looked upon with disfavor.

Playing with the wind. The following recommendations can help to maximize your advantage when playing with the wind:

1. When playing in a strong tailwind, develop the attitude that you must win every game—when receiving as well as when serving.
2. Swing more slowly and keep groundstrokes and volleys low so they do not go beyond the oppo-

nent's baseline. Be careful when attempting deep shots, since errors are easily produced with the wind at your back. Topspin can be effective, but only if carefully controlled.

3. Aim for a higher percentage of first serves, as the danger of double-faulting is greater.

4. Lobbing with the wind is risky, and sometimes futile, since the lob either tends to go long or affords the net man an opportunity to hit an overhead. Hit very few offensive lobs with the wind.

5. Allow your opponent's high lobs to bounce, since you will be swinging at a slower ball from a relatively shallow position in the court.

6. Do not hit drop shots, since your opponent will be able to return them without difficulty.

7. If your opponent, hitting against the wind, is coming to the net and winning a high percentage of points, try to take the net away from him by advancing to the forecourt behind any reasonable approach shot.

8. If your opponent is against the wind and is rarely coming to the net, and if you have solid groundstrokes, stay away from the net unless you have an easy approach shot. Win your points by outsteadying him.

Playing against the wind. If you are practicing with a player below your level in ability, try to play the entire match against the wind, as it will afford you a tougher workout.

Here are some tips to keep in mind when facing a strong headwind:

1. Since hitting against the wind is very tiring (harder swinging and quicker movements are required), avoid backcourt rallies unless the point is crucial or you are nearing the end of a match. To avoid extended baseline rallies, take more chances, either by hitting harder or by advancing to the net.

2. Do not allow the opponent's high lobs to bounce, since your smash will have to travel too great a distance to reach its target. In addition, the lob might bounce over the fence, not allowing you any play on the ball.

3. The drop shot can be used effectively when playing against the wind.

4. Hit your groundstrokes higher and harder than you normally would. (If you are a hard hitter who is playing against the wind, you will not be handicapped as much as the soft hitter. Powerful play-

ers often prefer hitting into the wind.)

5. Seldom use the American twist or the slow overspin service, as they tend to sit up, inviting disaster.

Playing in a crosscourt wind. Be sure you have the wind behind you if you are hitting a crosscourt shot (*Fig. 18.1*). If your opponent is at the net, pass him on the side of the court that the wind is blowing from (*Fig. 18.2*).

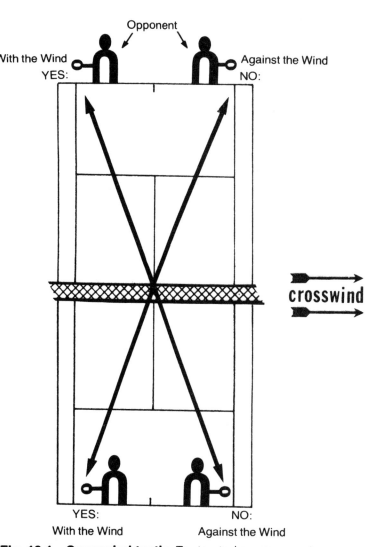

Fig. 18.1 Crosswind tactic. Try to stroke crosscourt with the wind. If opponent responds crosscourt, he will be stroking against the wind.

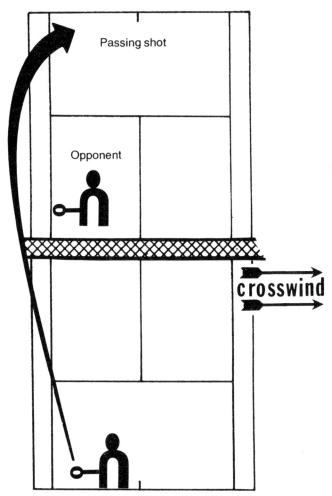

Passing shot

Opponent

crosswind

Fig. 18.2 When trying to pass the net man in a crosswind, hit the ball to the side the wind is blowing from.

3. Wear a hat with a peak to reduce glare. A light-colored and lightweight hat can also provide a feeling of coolness, and can protect you from sunburned and dried-out skin.
4. If you are uncomfortable wearing a hat, but want to reduce glare, apply antiglare black substance to the skin under your eyes.

Playing in shadow. When trees surround a tennis court, there will be shadows. Here are two brief recommendations for coping with a shadowy court:

1. Strive for power on serves and groundstrokes, since it is very difficult for your opponent to cope with pace on a shadowy court.
2. If part of your opponent's court is in shadow and part is not, aim toward the shadowed area.

Playing in fading light. For most working people, playing at dusk on weekdays is common practice. Here are some suggestions for twilight competition:

1. Do not lob if the sky is darkening, since your opponent can see the ball easily and might smash it away.
2. Try not to volley unless you have a "sitter," since you will not be able to see the ball well enough.
3. Serve as hard as possible, since the receiver needs adequate light to time fast balls.
4. Move farther behind your baseline to allow more time to focus on the opponent's oncoming shots. Incidentally, switching from white to the more visible yellow balls can add ten to fifteen minutes a day to your playing time.

Playing in hot weather. The following recommendations are for those competitors who are in poor physical condition:

1. In hot weather, extend points and prolong the match only if you are in much better shape than your opponent, or if you are doing much less running than he. Above all, know your physical limitations.
2. In hot weather, on clay courts, be very discreet about serving and volleying, since this is unusually fatiguing.
3. Do not chase wildly after all shots. Conserve your energy as much as possible.
4. Drink liquids during the match.

Playing in a strong sun. One disadvantage of playing indoors is that you do not learn to adjust to a blinding sun. The following four recommendations will help you cope with the sun.

1. When the sun is facing your opponent, use the lob frequently, to help nullify his net game and to force errors.
2. When looking into the sun as you serve, change the position of the toss to enable you to see the ball at contact. You can make your toss higher or lower, or farther to the left or right. If you cannot help being temporarily blinded, you will have to remain in the back of the court after serving.

5. Restrict day-of-the-match practice to a half hour or less, and keep the warmup short.
6. Wear light-colored clothing and a hat.
7. Try to sit during the one-minute changeover.
8. Schedule practice in the heat to develop physical and psychological stamina, but remember that it is extremely difficult to prepare fully for a gruelling match in the heat.

To get ready for the 1966 Italian Championships, I was playing five tough sets of singles a day, and doing roadwork. As it turned out, this training routine was nearly inadequate, since the temperature rose suddenly in Rome. In the first round I had been playing for three and a half hours when darkness forced the postponement of the match. We had completed only three sets and the contest was scheduled for the best of five. The match was very tough, and I had lost so much water that later in the evening, while dining in a restaurant, I fell from my chair with cramps. The next day we played two more sets in the steaming arena, and fortunately I won the marathon.

One year, in the Yugoslav Championships in Dubrovnik, it became so hot that the tournament referee thought it wisest to play all matches at eight o'clock in the morning. Due to my opponent's late arrival from a distant part of the country, my match was started at noon on a court that could be conservatively described as a blazing inferno. In such stifling heat on slow clay, a poorly conditioned player has *no* chance of winning against a steady baseliner. Through practice, you can at least partially prepare for these gruelling conditions.

Playing in cold weather. As some of you often play in temperatures below 60 or 65 degrees, I offer the following three bits of advice:

1. Start very slowly to avoid muscle pulls, and wear your warmup suit until you break a sweat.
2. Expect the ball to bounce lower and slower when it is cold.
3. Usually, there is little benefit in attempting to take advantage of an opponent's poor physical condition when the temperature is low.

Playing in Rain. Players in the Pacific Northwest region of the U.S. are constantly faced with a drizzle. Here are four brief recommendations for those who have to play in wet conditions:

1. On hard courts, a slight amount of moisture will cause balls to skid and come off the court faster than usual. Therefore, prepare your backswing earlier than usual.
2. On clay and grass courts, be prepared to swing harder to achieve your usual depth, since the balls become heavier.
3. If light rain is falling, use a racket with nylon strings, since gut frays and stretches when it becomes wet.
4. Playing on moist hard courts is dangerous, since the surface becomes very slippery. On clay courts a very light rain does not pose a traction problem.

In the next chapter I will deal with an aspect of tennis that is of paramount importance. The problem of changing tactics in the middle of the match is a delicate one, and well worth discussion.

Chapter 19

CHANGING TACTICS IN THE MIDDLE OF A MATCH

MAKE MINOR TACTICAL CHANGES CONTINUALLY

If you are alert in a match, you will continually evaluate your winning and losing shots as well as those of your opponent. You can appraise the situation by analyzing exactly how you are losing points. Let us say that on the first two points of the match you return the opponent's serve, and he answers with outright winners. You should first ask yourself the question, Why was he able to make putaways off of my two returns? You quickly realize that both of your returns of service were shallow. You should then say to yourself, "On the next point, I will try for more depth on my return so I don't get burned three times in a row." Or, if your opponent has put away three forehand volleys in the second game of the match, you should start to give his backhand volley a workout. These are but two examples of the types of small tactical changes you should make throughout a match.

There are other minor changes in strategy you can make during a tennis match. You can serve a little harder or softer, hit a little shorter or deeper (as in the example cited above), and hit stronger or more careful approach shots. Taking more time between points—but certainly not stalling—can have a positive effect on your game, and has to be viewed as a tactical option. Although changes of this nature can make a considerable difference in the outcome of a match, there is also a possibility that they will not make much of a difference at all. There are certain changes you can make, however, that will almost surely alter the course of a match—for better or for worse.

SHOULD YOU MAKE A MAJOR CHANGE DURING A MATCH?

What is a major change? If you have been playing a match from the backcourt and suddenly you start rushing to the net, this is a major change and probably will have an immediate effect on the outcome. If your opponent has only hit two volleys in the first set, and suddenly you start feeding him short balls and drop shots, causing him to hit five volleys in the first game of the second set, this is also a significant change. If you were playing a tactically normal tennis game, moving the opponent from side to side, and then you started lobbing every ball down the center of his court, this would constitute a major change.

"Always change a losing game, and never change a winning game." This is an oft-quoted expression. Its first part is fraught with danger and in need of qualification, whereas its second part is almost always true. One of the rare cases in which you might change tactics while winning is if your physical condition is poor and you cannot finish the match by playing long points. If you are winning, you would try not to change tactics; moreover, you should not alter *anything* affecting the rhythm of the match, including the time you take for the changeover.

Making a major tactical change when you are losing is often advisable, but it can be futile if you are incapable of playing that style of game to which you switch. For example, if you are losing points from the back of the court, but do not have an adequate volley, you have no choice but to remain in the backcourt. From the baseline, at least, you can offer moderate resistance. Any secondary game plan you attempt should be thoroughly tested in nonpressure practice situations.

Can your opponent sustain his good play? If you are playing your normal style of game as well as you can, a question to contemplate before making a major tactical change is, Can my opponent continue his high level of play? Knowing a player's past match record is helpful when this question comes up. Some players will be able to maintain a high standard of play indefinitely, and when this is the case, you have the ideal candidate against whom to make a major change.

There are other players who will be leading you in a match and against whom you should not drastically alter tactics. Some individuals can play an outstanding set, but cannot sustain a high level of play for an entire match. In these situations, the storm will probably blow over, and the "hot" players will revert to their normal level of play. You might be trailing a player because he has had more than his share of lucky breaks, such as hitting eight or ten balls on the line, or making some winning let-cords during a freakish first set. Other individuals become nervous, and have difficulty maintaining an aggressive style of play near the end of a match. A vivid example occurred in a match in Freudenstadt, Germany, where I lost the first set and trailed 2–5 in the second. The German became hesitant, and I got my foot in the door and won five games in a row, for the set; subsequently I won the match. Afterward, he heaved his racket over the fence and yelled, "Mein Gott!" This little village in the Black Forest had not heard so much commotion in many a year.

Your opponent's stamina. There are other factors to consider when making a major tactical change in your tennis game. There is nothing that can cause an opponent's precise, aggressive game to disintegrate faster than fatigue. Let us say, for example, your opponent is obviously not in good physical condition, or has a reputation for lacking stamina, and you are having lengthy backcourt exchanges. You have lost the first set six games to four. In this instance, it might be advisable for you to continue playing your same drawn-out game rather than starting an attack that would give him a breather.

When should a major change be made in a match? You should make a major change when you are reasonably sure that if you continue to play the same way, you will lose. It is often best to make the major change at the end of the first set, especially if you have been beaten badly. If you wait until the middle of the second set, after losing the first, it will likely be too late.

If you are losing badly in the first set, the last game or two can be used to drop-shot and work the opponent. At this point, if you play a loose shot or two (the drop shot is often a low-percentage play), he may interpret this as a sign that your resistance has broken down, and he may be lulled into a false sense of secu-

rity. If, however, at the beginning of the second set, you suddenly become tenacious as hell on every ball, you can produce nervousness and bewilderment in your opponent.

If you can, change tactics even before losing the first set. However, it can be difficult to discern how you will fare after only three or four games; you have not observed a sufficient sampling of points, and your conclusions can be questionable. For example, if you have an excellent serve-and-volley game, and your opponent has broken you early in the first set with some spectacular backhand-overspin passing shots, does it mean he is capable of doing this throughout the set? Perhaps if you served a little deeper and moved up to the net faster, he would almost never break you. Thus, you might use the second part of the first set (since you are behind in score anyway) to test your opponent with this tactical change.

Your opponent can copy your game and use it against you. There is some danger of introducing a new style of play or a new tactic against an opponent when you are winning. Some players will notice how effective your new strategy is, and will say to themselves, "He is working that new play very well against me; that isn't a bad idea; I think I'll use it on him." The new tactic could involve the use of a drop shot, or your looping the ball high in the air on groundstrokes, or your serving harder; it could even mean coming to the net on returns of service. The important point to remember is that if you are leading your opponent in a match, you should force *him* to make the change that could alter the equilibrium of the contest.

Try not to break your resolve. In a tough match we usually tend to play the particular style of game with which we have had success in the past. When contemplating a major tactical change in the middle of a tennis match, some players become tentative in carrying out their original plan or in using an alternate one. For some, changing strategy, or even thinking about doing so, can often be dangerous. Remember, whether you change tactics or not, play your chosen game with conviction, leaving no trace of doubt or hesitancy.

In this chapter we have been concerned with changing tactics in the middle of a match. In the next, we will explore the topic of altering tactics according to the score of the match.

Chapter 20

CHANGING TACTICS ACCORDING TO THE SCORE OF THE GAME, SET, AND MATCH

In a tennis match, should players treat all points the same, regardless of the score and conditions; give one hundred percent, physically and mentally; play the high-percentage shot, to try to win each point? The answer is a definite *no,* and for several reasons.

PLAYING MORE THAN ONE MATCH IN A DAY

In most weekend adult tournaments you have to play more than one match a day. In 1972, in the Western Massachusetts Championship on slow clay, I had the *misfortune* of reaching the finals of singles and doubles, and was forced to play *eleven* matches over a two-day period. (I had no grounds to be upset, since the rules were spelled out long before the tournament started.) In cases such as this, which are not unusual, running your tail off on every point would be nothing short of suicidal. In these situations, you should know when to exert yourself and when to coast. From the physical standpoint, it is impossible for most of us to go "flat out" for every ball, especially against a tough opponent in hot and slow conditions.

TIRING THE OPPONENT

There are instances when you might deliberately attempt to tire the opponent rather than win the point. For example, if you find yourself 4–0 or 5–1 down in the first set, you will want to tire your opponent as much as possible with drop shots or angled balls. In addition, there is always the possibility that if you have sufficiently broken his rhythm, you may win the first set yourself. Then, at the start of the second set, you should go all out with your high-percentage game.

USE YOUR WEAK SHOTS AS A DIVERSIONARY TACTIC

There are shots in the repertoire of every player that are not as effective as others in winning points. For example, you might win only 55 percent of the points in which you use a flat service, whereas when you serve with overspin your winning-point percentage rises to 70. Nevertheless, you should continue to incorporate the flat serve in your arsenal, since its change of pace makes the overspin even more effective. By utilizing this diversionary tactic, you can make it difficult for the opponent to become grooved by not feeding him the same menu of shots. The correct time to use lower-percentage shots is during less important points or games.

GAINING A PSYCHOLOGICAL EDGE

A valuable result of utilizing low-percentage shots on unimportant points is the effect this tactic can have on the morale of the opponent. When an opponent wins a considerable number of insignificant points, but is restricted to a much lower percentage in winning crucial points, he has a tendency to become discouraged. He is inclined to harbor thoughts such as, "I am winning a lot of points, but I don't understand why he's ahead of me in games." Also, you can benefit psychologically by knowing you have reserve power that can be called upon at those times you are not weaving him into your tactical web with "irrelevant" and low-percentage shots.

TACTICS WITH VASTLY SUPERIOR PLAYERS

Occasionally you will encounter a player who is completely out of your class in tennis ability. When competing against such a talented individual, you would be wise not to use many low-percentage shots. There have been a few rather unfortunate occasions when I have met an international-class player who was having a hot hand, and though I was leading 40–15 and playing high-percentage shots continually, I had only a 50-percent chance of winning the game. Although it is nice to be perpetually optimistic, there are cases such as this in which victory is out of the question, and winning two games a set amounts to a moral victory.

In summary, you should place points in the following three categories:

1. Points you go all out to win
2. Points that are used to tire the opponent
3. Points that are used as variations on your "bread-and-butter" attack.

You should always play a point with one of these purposes in mind.

WHICH ARE THE IMPORTANT AND THE LESS-IMPORTANT POINTS IN A GAME?

The following categorization of points is based upon the premise that all points do not have equal value:

Important Points	Less-Important Points	Least-Important Points
First	30–0	40–0
Second	0–30	0–40
15–all	40–15	
30–15	15–40	
15–30		
30–all		
40–30		
30–40		
Deuce		
Advantage In		
Advantage Out		

As you can see from these categories, "Important Points" are those in which either the game score is even or one of the players is only one point ahead. With a little effort, either player can get on top of his opponent and win the game. Since I have placed eleven categories of points in the "important" class, it is obvious that I believe a player should fight hard and play percentage tennis during most points of a match.

In the second category, "Less-Important Points," there is a difference of two points between players, whereas in the "Least-Important Points," there is a three-point spread between them. When you are two or three points behind, it usually takes a strong effort, and some luck, to win the game. If you are behind 0–40, and you set your mind on winning the game, you will invariably frustrate yourself in the attempt. Be tough, dogged, and relentless throughout a match, but be discriminating when you launch a herculean effort when far behind in score during a game or set.

WHAT ARE THE IMPORTANT GAMES IN A SET?

Following is a categorization of games according to their significance within the set:

Important Games	Less-Important Games	Least-Important Games
First	3–0	4–0
Second	0–3	0–4
Third	4–1	5–0
2–1	1–4	0–5
1–2	5–2	5–1
3–1	2–5	1–5
1–3		
2–all		
3–2		
2–3		
4–2		
2–4		
3–all		
4–3		
3–4		
5–3		
3–5		
4–all		
5–4		
4–5		
5–all		
6–5		
5–6		
6–all (tiebreaker)		

Listed in the "Important" category are games of equal score, or scores in which one of the players is either ahead or behind by one or two games. In these situations, a service break can instantly turn the momentum of the match around.

In the "Important" category I would also add all match games (one game away from winning the match), since they can be important psychological turning points. Even if you are 4–0 or 5–0 ahead in the second set after having won the first, bear down hard and get your opponent off the court as quickly as possible. Understandably, every game in the final set is important.

In the "Less-Important Games" category there is a three-game spread between the players, and holding or breaking service one time will not be sufficient to bring the trailing player up to even terms.

In the category of "Least-Important Games" one of the players is four or five games ahead of the other. In these instances it is extremely difficult for the person behind in score to win the set, so a gargantuan physical and mental effort should be used only if you are in the final set, or in the second set, having lost the first.

WHAT ARE THE IMPORTANT SETS IN A MATCH?

Naturally, the final set in a match is of paramount importance, as it decides the outcome. The first set is extremely important because if you win it, some opponents will not fight as hard afterward. After losing the first set, some opponents realize in order to win they must remain on the court for a long time. They might not look forward to this.

If you are fortunate enough to win the first set, do not become complacent. Bear down very hard in the first two or three games of the second set, since when some opponents fall behind, they will lose composure, and resort to low-percentage strategies.

Let us now proceed from the area of important and unimportant points, games, and sets to a topic of concern to any aspiring tennis player. How should the practicing of tennis be viewed in comparison with participation in tournaments?

Chapter **21**

TACTICS USED IN TOURNAMENTS AND IN PRACTICE MATCHES

In this chapter we will differentiate between tactics used in practice matches and those used in tournament-type tennis, such as in interscholastic, intercollegiate, and interclub matches.

TOURNAMENT TENNIS

How do tournaments benefit a player? Why are tournaments essential for the aspiring and serious-minded tennis player? Do players have justification in traveling hundreds of miles to play in tournaments that offer no prize money? Following is a list of the main benefits of participating in higher-level competition:

1. A tournament player is exposed to various courts, balls, and conditions which season his talents. The player who has never experienced different types of surfaces and who confines tennis to his club or to one set of courts will not develop into a mature tennis player.
2. Tournaments help a player become accustomed to spectators. With experience he will be able to maintain poise and concentration while others watch him.
3. A player can always ascertain his own ability by playing in tournaments. In addition, others can judge a tennis player by what he has accomplished in tournaments. In terms of a player's reputation, practice-match results are almost meaningless. Tournament scores provide the documentation for the ranking of players, and tennis rankings are quite accurate in their judgment of performance and ability. Other types of performers cannot be looked at as objectively, and as a result are more likely to foster delusions of grandeur. Not so with tournament tennis players.
4. Tournaments are helpful in revealing a player's specific weaknesses. He then knows what strokes he should try to improve in practice.
5. Tournaments provide a variety of opponents and high-level competition. Such competition can be scarce in practice, since, in some locales, lining up skillful opposition can be difficult. One often encounters many good players in tournaments, and no player in history became great without first having lengthy tournament exposure.
6. Tournaments afford the participants the satisfaction of playing a match to its conclusion. Because of the public-tennis-court shortage, many practice matches last only forty-five minutes to an hour, and, as a result, go unfinished.
7. Tournaments can reward a player in terms of victories, prizes, and rankings, and they can also motivate him to want to work on his game in practice.
8. Tournaments offer abundant opportunities for socializing. Renewing acquaintances and meeting new friends is, in my opinion, the greatest benefit of tournament tennis.

What are the disadvantages of tournaments? Playing in tournaments is not, by any means, desirable activity for many players. Following is a list of the main drawbacks of playing in tournaments:

1. Tournaments are time-consuming. They involve filling out entry forms, traveling considerable distances, and waiting around for the playing of delayed matches.
2. Tournaments are costly. They involve high entry fees, and transportation and lodging costs. There is prize money in some tournaments, but for the vast majority of players, financial remuneration is not commensurate with the effort required to develop a fine tennis game. The rewards of tennis, for practically all of us, are basically nonmaterial in nature. In addition, the physical and psychological toll of fighting through five or six rounds of a tournament can be high.

3. In tournaments, a player cannot experiment with new shots in a carefree and spontaneous manner. In using proved and carefully calculated strokes and patterns, a tournament-tennis match becomes a test of discipline.

4. There is more tension in tournaments than in practice matches. Newspapers and magazines often report the scores, rankings are involved, invitations to special events are occasionally at stake, and prize money can be up for grabs. Nevertheless, there are a few players who thrive on the tension and excitement of tournament tennis; they love to be watched by spectators, and enjoy any kind of publicity as well.

Since tournaments are a showcase for your tennis game, it stands to reason you should not enter them unless you have been playing regularly, and are physically fit. If you are playing as well as you can, you might enjoy competing, even if you lose in the first round.

PRACTICE-MATCH TENNIS

Although tournaments bring the element of maturity to a player's tennis game, they do not develop the basic strokes. The rudiments of the game are learned far from the electrically charged surroundings of tournaments. It is in the serene and quiet atmosphere of practice sessions that great tennis games are created and nurtured.

If you are serious about tennis, your practice routine should involve both the playing of sets and drilling on specific shots. Drilling with a large number of balls enables a player to stroke many more shots in a given period of time than does playing sets.

The following are specific practice-match recommendations to make your game more effective:

1. Establish a winning habit in practice matches. When playing practice matches with inferior players, first guarantee you will win by jumping off to a lead, and *then* start experimenting with new tactics. Providing you win, it should not matter how many points, games, or sets you drop along the way.

   However, in the case in which you are undertaking a major grip or stroke change, have no fear of losing in practice, or possibly even in tournaments. When undergoing radical changes, a person's tennis game usually goes far below its

normal level. Then, after weeks and months and possibly years of competition, the change unleashes the potential for better play. It is up to you if you wish to make the sacrifice of time.

2. Develop new strokes and strategies in practice. Always work on one or two tactical plans or shots in practice matches. Do not simply play practice matches as you would tournament contests. Some of your experimenting might involve developing an attacking return of service, hitting an overspin-backhand down the line, working on a serve with less spin, hitting all strokes harder, or developing a drop shot.

3. Use the overload principle in practice to develop physical fitness for tournaments. Develop practice routines that force you to work longer and harder than you do in tournament matches. Try to supplement your practice sessions with some running, especially if your on-court practice workouts are not too demanding. Once in a while it is a good idea to play the best of five sets, and try not to sit down during the changeover. It is also well for you to meet tougher players in practice.

4. Enjoy your practice sessions. Do not play with individuals who are personally offensive, and do not saddle yourself with a practice routine that is so physically torturous that it becomes repulsive.

5. Try to schedule different types of stylists for practice matches. For example, try to schedule a hard hitter, then a soft hitter, or a net rusher, then a baseliner.

6. Try to prevent "match staleness"; engage in a variety of drills. This condition of lethargy and fatigue is often caused by the playing of too many sets. In the majority of cases, being "overtennised" shows a lack of intelligent planning of practice sessions.

7. Do not worry about playing with new balls each session unless you are a tournament player, or unless you have ample money to do so. But do not use dead balls either (for example, pressure-packed balls out of the can for more than three or four weeks) for the playing of sets or for drilling.

8. Remember, if you are planning to enter a tennis tournament that is to be held on medium-fast courts, try to prepare for the tournament on an equally fast or a faster surface.

A book on tactics would be incomplete without a section on stamina. The next two chapters deal with lack of stamina, either on your part or your opponent's.

Chapter 22

ENERGY-SAVING TACTICS

Stamina and the lack of it play an important role wherever competitive tennis is played, and especially in warm and humid areas of the world. On clay courts in the southern and eastern U.S., in Southern Europe, and in many parts of Asia and Africa, the outcome of tennis matches relies on much more than strokes and concentration. Anyone who has played extensively in tournaments or club matches has been faced with the problem of fatigue. Certainly, as we age, we face this predicament with even greater frequency.

The problem I shall address in this chapter is, how do we cope with fatigue at any age? What do we do when we find ourselves in the middle of a match and without energy? What can the older player do to minimize exhaustion?

It would be improper to discuss match fatigue without first suggesting ways you can prevent it from occurring. (Chapter 3, "Match-Preparation Tactics," covers the latter subject in greater detail.)

STEPS TO PREVENT EXHAUSTION BEFORE THE MATCH BEGINS

1. Work out strenuously, six or seven times a week, when preparing for a tournament. Engage in tough practice matches so that tournaments will not seem unusually gruelling, physically or mentally. Practice against good players, since they will work you the hardest. Schedule some practice matches for the best of five sets, even though the tournament might schedule the best of three. Run two or three miles every other day, and then do quick starts and sprints. Run backward as well as forward. For me, this regimen has paid dividends, and in tournaments I have outlasted many players who had superior strokes.

2. If the match scheduled is likely to be played in high temperature and humidity, and you are slated to go against a formidable opponent, do not hit earlier the same day. If you feel you must have a workout, try to give yourself at least four or five hours of rest after perhaps a thirty-minute warmup.

(I remember once, in Austria, being scheduled on a hot day for a one-P.M. tournament-singles match. I was asked by the referee if I would not mind playing a mixed-doubles match first, at ten A.M. When I queried the official regarding my singles opponent's ability, he replied, "Oh, he is nothing—just the local baker." Being in excellent physical condition, and attempting to be cordial, I agreed to play the mixed-doubles match beforehand. It goes without saying that the match lasted almost three hours; I had had to take the majority of the shots, and to do most of the running. It was about one P.M. when we wearily walked off the court—the exact time the singles match was scheduled. I was given a forty-five-minute break for lunch. Upon returning, I went to the slow clay court and hit a few warmup balls with the "baker." I immediately realized I had no chance to win the match in my condition, since running fast and far was a necessary part of my game. I lost the match. As it turned out, the "local baker" was a ranked Austrian player. Had I been fresh, the match would have been difficult, but most probably I would have won. After that experience, I was a little less agreeable about playing doubles before my singles matches.)

3. Get a good night's sleep beforehand. If you do not have sound rest the night before a rough singles match on a hot day, your chances of winning will be lessened considerably.

4. On the day of the match, eat easily digestible food that supplies plenty of energy. Allow an hour or two between the time you finish eating, and the time you walk onto the court.

5. Older players should think about taking the following measures: using light-headed rackets;

using less topspin on groundstrokes, since top-spin strokes require more energy; taking shorter backswings on groundstrokes.

STEPS TO CONSERVE ENERGY DURING A MATCH

Following are specific tactics to use during a match in order to conserve strength and expend as little energy as possible:

1. Sip water, Gatorade, tea, or Coke during the match.
2. Sit down, preferably in the shade, during the one-minute changeover period. If there is shade at one end of the court, but not near the net post, sit in the shade.
3. Attempt to meet the ball earlier, and play most balls on or inside the baseline (Fig. 22.1).
4. Finish unimportant points faster by hitting just a

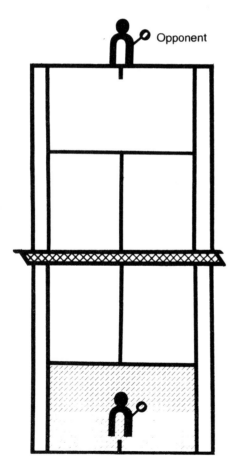

Opponent

Fig. 22.1 When you are tired, play points in the backcourt area.

little harder and taking more of a risk. The player who hits with very good pace does not have to run as fast or as far as the one who hits softly.

5. Take as much time between points as possible without stalling and irritating your opponent. The "code," referred to in the USTA rules, says walking to retrieve a distant third ball between points is stalling, so make sure you do this only at the end of games. The worst "help" you can receive when tired is the assignment of ball boys to your match! When they are running around, you do not get a reprieve in picking up balls.
6. Wear a light-colored hat with a visor, and a white and lightweight perforated shirt.
7. Do not sprint long distances for balls when you would only have a one chance in three or four of even touching them, much less winning the point.
8. If you are winning the match, and holding service by rushing to the net, conserve your energy on the games your opponent serves. Save almost everything for your own service games.
9. Volley from a deep position around the service line, not from on top of the net. Five or six break-neck sprints from the baseline to the net might be equivalent in energy expenditure to fifteen lei-surely approaches to the midcourt area. Also, by positioning yourself in the middle of the court, you will not be forced to rush back fast to cover lobs.
10. Slow down on first services in order to put a higher percentage of balls in play. A first-service fault means wasted energy. If you desire, you can even bounce your ball two or three times before serving, to gain additional rest.
11. When both you and your opponent are in the back of the court, you can try hitting your drives slower and higher above the net. Provided your opponent does not come in and volley your float-ers, you might have more time to recover be-tween strokes.
12. Breathe deeply between points. (However, if you are playing in smog in Los Angeles, breath-ing deeply is one of the worst tactical moves you can make, since you could become nauseous.)
13. If you are doing a great deal of running, and are not in superior shape compared with your oppo-nent, make sure that you are ahead in score. Change tactics immediately if you are working harder than your opponent *and losing.*

Chapter 23

TACTICS WHEN YOUR OPPONENT IS IN POOR PHYSICAL CONDITION

Although endurance can vary considerably from player to player, in most tournament matches played today, stamina does not play a major role in the outcome. First of all, most tournament competitors are in reasonably good physical condition; it is the nontournament player who is more likely to be woefully out of shape. Second, many tournament matches are played in moderate temperatures, such as those of the coastal areas of California, or indoors, where the temperature is usually controlled. Taking advantage of superior stamina is difficult if the temperature is below 85 and humidity is not high. Third, with the advent of tiebreakers that can conclude sets either at six-all or at eight-all, marathon matches are becoming a rarity.

Many colleges in the U.S. are even using no-ad scoring, in which the first player to earn four points wins the game. Traditionally, in women's, boys', and senior men's matches a short rest period is granted at the end of two sets.

Best-of-three-set matches played on hard courts, grass, or wood do not ordinarily require the endurance powers of a long-distance runner. But when a match is played on clay, and high temperatures and humidity enter the picture, an entirely different circumstance presents itself. An opponent with inferior endurance can be taken advantage of. The following suggestions are geared toward the adversary who has superior strokes and who would defeat you under normal conditions.

Signs of a lack of stamina. One good way to get information about an opponent's staying power, or lack of it, is to ask other players he has competed against. The following conditions can be signs of loss of stamina in an opponent:

1. Overweight.
2. Older age. At thirty or thiry-five years of age, a player does not have the same energy he had at twenty. After forty-five, he loses even more vigor.

3. Pale skin. Although this can be a sign of lack of stamina, it can also be misleading, since an opponent can be doing his roadwork and his practicing late in the afternoon or in the early morning. (There is also a possibility that he does not tan at all!)
4. Redness in the face.
5. Heavy breathing.
6. Excessive sweating.
7. Making an unforced error or two when previously he had not.
8. Taking excessive time between points and during the changeover.

TACTICS TO USE AGAINST A POORLY CONDITIONED OPPONENT

Let us now assume your opponent is vulnerable to fatigue, or is already tired. The question then becomes, Are *you* in excellent condition, and will you be able to benefit by turning the match into an endurance contest? Taking for granted the answer is in the affirmative, we will now go over the steps you can take to beat the opponent with superior shots but inferior physical conditioning.

1. Lengthen the warmup. Allow him to hit any shot he wants indefinitely, and do not rush the preliminaries along. (Do not irritate your opponent, however.) Most experienced opponents who lack endurance will move the warmup along rapidly. Recently I played a match against a fine-stroking but out-of-condition opponent who did his utmost to end the warmup as soon as it began. He not only moved the prelude along as quickly as possible; he stood under a tree against the back fence as he warmed up! He would take the ball

on the second, third, and even fourth bounce. Under these conditions, developing any type of rhythm was impossible. Since he gave me any shot I needed to be loosened up, I had no legitimate basis for complaint. Ultimately, I won the match. But I had lost the warmup!

2. If your opponent has superior guns but inferior stamina, do not be afraid to lose the first set in order to execute your tactic of working him over.

3. Continually hit toward the open part of the court to force the opponent to move. Do not hit behind the opponent, since he will not have to run as far. Hit the ball at moderate speed, and try to take it a little earlier in order to force him to move faster.

4. If you have a drop shot, use it, and follow it up with a lob *(Fig. 23.1)*.

5. Play a baseline game and prolong the rallies. (However, on crucial points, if you have a "sitter," put it away.) When the opponent comes to the net, lob and hit slow dinks to make him stretch. Do not stroke hard passing shots.

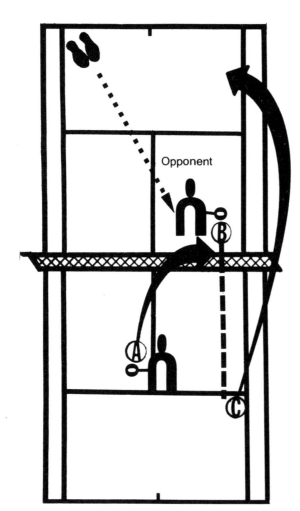

Order of shots
A. Drop shot
B. Opponent returns
C. Lob

Fig. 23.1 The drop-shot-and-lob combination tires an opponent.

Some years ago, I was scheduled to play a quarter-final match in the men's 35-years-and-over division of the Pacific Southwest tennis tournament in Los Angeles. My opponent had just been released from prison, where he had served a sentence for passing bad checks. He had the distinction of playing number one on an excellent prison tennis team, having beat out his sidekick, a convicted murderer, for the top spot. When the prison court was occupied, they had plenty of wall space to practice their shots!

Anyway, this fellow had a fine reputation as a tennis player. He played Wimbledon and other notable tournaments, and held a high U.S. ranking. I noticed he was carrying extra weight on his torso (although he had strong legs), and it was a hot day in September, so I decided to lengthen points. I did not think I could cope with him stroke for stroke.

The match started, and I worked him (and myself) hard for the first few games. At about two–all, he called over to his friend and requested a vodka tonic. I thought I was imagining this, or dreaming, but sure enough, a couple of minutes later the friend arrived with the alcoholic beverage. My opponent drank it rather quickly, and then proceeded to ask for an encore. As the match progressed he ordered another and another.

Meanwhile, I lost the first set, 6–4, and was feeling the physical effects of the match at about three–all in the second set. I decided to gamble by closing points out and coming to the net. Fortunately, my tactics were successful, and I won the second set.

I thought that after consuming four popcorn-box-size vodka tonics, my opponent would not be in any condition to play a third set, but how wrong I was! He started scampering around the court like it was the first game of the match, and proceeded to handle my case. I later discovered that he regularly imbibed during his matches. Perhaps the moral of the story is that appearances can deceive, or, in practical tennis terms, be careful with whom you try to lengthen points. Some tennis players would have hung their rackets up permanently after losing to a fat guy who had just got out of prison and who had downed several mixed drinks during the match. (I am happy to report that this amiable and talented player is presently doing well.)

Although the opponent who was just mentioned was good, he was still near my level in tennis ability. Eventually we will confront players who are far better than we or who are considerably below our level as a player. And dealing with these two categories of opponents is the subject of the next chapter.

Chapter 24

TACTICS AGAINST BETTER PLAYERS AND AGAINST INFERIOR PLAYERS

In tennis there are definite and distinct classes of playing ability. Since a great number of shots are exchanged in a match, ability and class predominate in determining the outcome. True upsets are almost nonexistent, since a player of one class rarely beats a player of another class.

I would define a "class" as a specific level of play whereby one player should regularly and decisively defeat another. According to this definition, there are probably a minimum of twelve or thirteen completely different levels of tennis skill.

All of us have faced, or will face, the predicament of playing a superior player, one out of our class. Even Tilden, Kramer, and Budge have faced the situation, at some time, in which, barring injury to the opponent, there was no chance of their winning. To use poker terms, the match was a "lock" even before the first point was played. Let us discuss the tactics we should use when we attempt to assault a veritable lion's den while armed with a butterfly net.

FACING THE BETTER PLAYER

Benefits of facing a better player. You are fortunate when you have the opportunity to play a better player, since it usually helps your game. You learn new ideas and pick up tips. For example, Roy Emerson felt his forehand improved each time he practiced with Pancho Segura, because the latter's two-handed forehand was so powerful and so well executed. (In this case, I am not implying that Segura is the better player.) A better player forces you to be more consistent, and quickly penalizes you when you hit short balls. He also tends to work you harder. When a player is giving you a rough time, you are often forced to change tactics and to exercise the mental aspect of your game. Finally, the superior player makes you acutely aware of the true strengths of and glaring weaknesses in your game.

Two disadvantages in competing with a better player are that you lose whenever you play him, and that you are not allowed the extravagance of practicing your low-percentage and exciting shots. You have an accepted obligation to offer maximum resistance to a more skilled opponent.

Tactics to use against the better player. Hit no harder than you normally do. The worst possible strategy is to blast balls beyond your level of ability to do so. The most incorrect assumption you can make is that you must do something spectacular to remain competitive. Try to prepare faster, move more quickly to the ball, and concentrate very hard when you stroke. Play percentage tennis and do not attempt unreliable shots.

Although you should play within your capabilities, you can still vary your game. You can elect to stroke a little harder or softer, hit high loops from the back of the court, come to the net or stay at the baseline.

Pay particular attention to the better player's physical condition. If you can keep him out on the court long enough and tire him, you might slide your foot in the door. This is about your only hope of eking out a victory against a player with superior strokes.

Your mental state when playing the better player. Before the match, you should feel free of pressure, since no one is expecting you to win, and you have everything to gain and very little to lose. You must adopt the proper mental attitude as you approach a match. Otherwise, you can find yourself very disappointed at the outcome.

One year I was playing the circuit on the French Riviera, and entered the Cannes Lawn Tennis Club tournament. I was slated to play singles, and entered the doubles as well, with a personal friend. He was scheduled to play his first-round singles match at ten A.M. on a Tuesday against a "tiger" from the French Davis Cup team. A few days before the match my friend began to place bets on himself (with odds, of course) that he would beat this seeded player. My friend's prematch prophesies caused considerable talk among the players, and they looked forward to this event. The day of the big match arrived, but I was unable to attend because of some business matters. At about noon, an hour before our one-o'clock doubles match was to begin, I arrived at the club and found out the score. The Frenchman won very easily, as most of the gang had expected. My friend was so discouraged with the result, and so uncomfortable in the situation he had created, that he skipped our doubles match without even telling me about his change of plans. Apparently, within an hour after he lost, he left town, and that same afternoon flew out of the country as well. I did not know what had happened to him until four months later when I saw him dragging into our chalet in Kitzbühel, Austria. He had decided to return to the tournament circuit. During this interval he had won two impressive trophies, the tennis championship of Cyprus, and a lovely wife he had met in Israel.

Remember—having confidence is fine, but pressuring yourself into a false state of overconfidence can bring on disillusionment and disappointment.

There are some positive thoughts to entertain when tangling with a superior player. The following is such an example: "His good reputation is not going to win him any points; he is going to have to prove his ability on the court. He will not receive any gifts from me, and I will force him to make winning shots."

Eventually, we are all going to be faced with opponents so strong that our winning the match or even a set might be out of the question. Winning *games* can almost be impossible. When confronted with such overwhelming strength, enter the match with the attitude that you will work him as hard as possible, and you will win as many *points* as you are able. At these times, take pride in your game, especially your defense, and fight your opponent all the way, even if the score winds up 6–0 6–1 against you. Make yourself a problem to him, and do not surrender mentally. We

can be discouraged, but we should never quit. There are times when winning only two games a set should be considered an accomplishment.

Asking a better player for a game. In tennis we usually do not ask a player far out of our class for a game. It is unfair to him. If you think you can get three games in a set, then it is perfectly all right to invite him to play. If when playing this match you lose 6–3 6–3, you could state your availability for a return engagement, but allow him the privilege of extending the actual invitation. Sometimes, a better player will want to practice with you because he can use the session as a proving ground for certain shots. Often, you can be an excellent drilling partner for him. Always allow the stronger player the privilege of directing the practice action, whether it be drilling or playing sets.

FACING THE INFERIOR PLAYER

Most of the comments pertaining to the better player can be applied here, but in reverse. However, I would like to add a couple of remarks. Have respect for but do not fear the player who is in a class below yours. Be secure in knowing that ability will determine the outcome of the contest.

In a tournament match, attempt to defeat the inferior player as quickly as possible. If you are capable of winning 6–2 6–2, bear down and beat him by those scores.

In a tournament match, once you break your opponent down and force him to miss, do not allow him to regain confidence and rhythm during that match. Once you have taken the lead and are dominating the match, do not relax and let your opponent get his "foot back in the door." This could be comparable to having to defeat two opponents in one match.

You will likely have other categories of opponents besides those who are not in your ability class. I am referring to senior competitors, juniors, and female players. Each of these groups of players has physical limitations that can be taken advantage of by the thinking tennis player.

Chapter 25

TACTICS WHEN OPPOS-ING SENIOR, WOMEN, AND JUNIOR PLAYERS

This brief chapter is primarily intended for the special but not uncommon situation of the average male player's being confronted by senior, women, and junior players.

TACTICS AGAINST SENIOR PLAYERS

The first thing to remember is that trying to out-steady older men and women can be very difficult, since their strokes might have become well grooved. As the years go by, players tend to smooth out their strokes. Since older players are slower than their younger counterparts, force them to move, providing you have the stroking ability. You might be able to make outright placements or to force them into errors after maneuvering them into poor position. Volleying can be an effective strategy, since older players usually cannot move quickly to the ball. In short, taking advantage of an older player's slowness is the first basic tactic.

A second tactic is to whittle away at his stamina. However, do not count too heavily on a severe loss of strength, since some men and women of forty, and even into their sixties, stay fit and have good endurance. To exploit a player's stamina you must move him around the court, using, if possible, the drop shot and the lob. If your objective is to deplete energy, the ball should be kept in play as long as possible. Taking your groundstrokes from on or inside the baseline (i.e., as close to "on the rise" as possible) will usually guarantee that the opponent will work harder, providing you can minimize your errors.

TACTICS AGAINST WOMEN PLAYERS

A woman tennis player's biggest weakness is not lack of power. Except on the serve and the overhead, many women can equal the pace of some advanced male players. It is a woman's relative inability to move quickly that leaves her vulnerable on a tennis court. I have played some high-ranking women, including world champions, and none of them could cover the court like men.

How does one take advantage of this lack of speed? You can come to the net, and you can drop-shot. Chris Evert, who in my opinion is the greatest woman player to ever set foot on a clay court, loses to a fellow who is not even ranked in the top ten in the state of Florida. What is his success based upon? He uses the drop shot with great effect in order to avoid what could be a sticky baseline-to-baseline battle.

The second-most-effective tactic to use against women is to advance to the net and direct volleys away from them. A good approach shot or serve has to be made to set up the volley. Women often will not be able to reach volleys that many men can run down easily. The worst tactic you can use against most tournament-level female players is to stay in the back of the court and hit normal deep groundstrokes.

Incidentally, the previous remarks are not intended to detract from the quality of women's tennis. Their play is interesting, and constantly improving. In another decade to two, as greater athletes take up the game, we are going to witness a remarkable jump in the ability level of women's tennis.

TACTICS AGAINST JUNIOR PLAYERS

Very young junior players should be played similarly to women. In addition to taking advantage of their lack of speed by volleying the ball, it is also advisable to bring them to the net with drop shots. I have seen twelve- and thirteen-year-olds who hit all shots extremely well but who, because of their lack of reach at the net, were unable to generate substantial offense until they reached sixteen or seventeen years of age. Small people can be easily passed while they are at the net, and also easily lobbed.

Another effective tactic to use against juniors, or against small adults, is the semilob, or loop shot, when both of you are behind your baselines. Unless a short player takes this ball on the rise, he will be forced to stroke it from above his head.

Some youngsters have extremely sound strokes and are very steady from the back of the court. Once, when Dick Stockton was eleven years old and I was playing in men's tournaments, we drilled with forehands crosscourt, and I found that he had more depth and consistency than I did. But this is the exception. On average, the older player will prevail through greater steadiness. This is the older player's plus.

We have been discussing players whom we can exploit on the court. The next chapter will deal with that maverick of a tennis player who might exploit us by using unsportsmanlike tactics. We must be ready to deal with the unethical player if we are to be effective tournament competitors.

Chapter 26

TACTICS AGAINST UNETHICAL PLAYERS

Since very little is written on this subject, and it is seldom discussed, even experienced tournament players are often perplexed when faced with unethical opponents. Tennis players have difficulty coping in this area because they are somewhat confused themselves as to what is and what is not proper conduct on the court. This topic touches upon interpersonal relationships, psychology, fair play, and a knowledge of the rules. The remarks that follow are intended to shed some light on the shadowy domain of tennis ethics.

UNDERLYING ASSUMPTIONS IN QUESTIONS OF ETHICS

Any discussion of such a touchy question as whether a ball is in or out must be done in a *courteous* and *rational* manner. We usually extract decent behavior from opponents if we treat them decently. Since one of the prime purposes of tennis is to create and maintain friendships, polite behavior should prevail.

We also must be aware that in a tournament-tennis match there is a likelihood that one or both parties will be a little nervous. Players tend to be edgy in competitive surroundings. Compound this with the fact that tournament players might not be friends, as practice partners are, and you can see the necessity for behaving discreetly.

There is considerable responsibility placed on the shoulders of tournament competitors in the U.S., since, in the majority of tournaments, unlike in European competition, players must call the balls that land on their side of the net. Aside from the relatively few big-time tennis events with prize money, most American tournaments do not utilize umpires until the semifinal or final rounds.

In my opinion, if we are to develop into good sportsmen and sportswomen, we should have feedback on our poor behavior. We all make mistakes, but if we are to grow in self-understanding, we must be receptive to suggestions and cues from other individuals.

We must also help to educate others on the tennis court, and, if possible, avoid hurting them. For example, carrying a tale of an opponent's poor calls back to the locker room or clubhouse is not the most discreet activity. A direct discussion of the incident with the individual involved will help us advance in "tennis maturity," and, in the case of an antagonist's transgressions, will help guarantee us from being unfairly taken advantage of in a match.

It is imperative that fairness prevail in tennis competition, and that the winner be determined on sheer playing ability. Neither player should be allowed to take unfair advantage by circumventing the written or unwritten rules.

The following are specific and troublesome areas in which I will attempt to distinguish correct behavior from that which is incorrect.

THE OPPONENT WHO IS LATE

When a match is scheduled for a given hour, we should make every attempt to be there at precisely that hour. This is in deference to our opponent as well as to the tournament committee. When our lateness is going to exceed fifteen or twenty minutes, if at all possible we should notify the tournament desk or the proper authority. There are going to be instances in which someone has been delayed, and we should take this into account while waiting for a tardy opponent. If, however, you are scheduled against an opponent who is habitually late, then it is often wise, and well within your prerogative, to demand a default after twenty-five or thirty minutes. Also, in cases in which you have made important appointments following the match, you should have no qualms about defaulting an opponent who shows up an hour late. The worst situation is when you have the feeling that you must hurry the match in order to make an appointment. As a general rule, defaults hurt both parties, and should be avoided whenever possible.

THE OPPONENT WHO TAKES TOO LONG, OR NOT LONG ENOUGH, TO WARM UP

Chapter 4 describes the normal ingredients for a tennis-match warmup. The average and accepted warmup time is about ten to fifteen minutes. If both parties agree there should be no warmup, that is fine. If both players want to prolong the limbering-up period to twenty or twenty-five minutes, providing there is no backlog of matches, that is also acceptable. When warming up, even if you are tired, you have an obligation to give your opponent the shots he wants within the aforementioned normal boundaries.

After a three-minute warmup you should not be asked by your opponent if you are ready to play. This forces you to take a defensive position that is unfair. Your reply to such a question should simply be, "No, I would like to take a normal warmup." If, after another minute, he asked, "Are you ready to play?" you could ask, "Are you tired?" If he says yes, then say, "I will try to make this as short as possible, but I don't want to risk injury by shortening the loosening-up period." If he persists, I would ask that he furnish a surrogate for the warmup, or I would make an appeal to the referee. Hardly ever should these latter steps be necessary.

If your opponent seems to be prolonging the warmup, you have every right to ask, after fifteen minutes, "Are you ready for the serves?" If the warmup lasts longer than twenty minutes, you have ample justification to ask the referee to have the match started.

THE COMPULSIVE TALKER, OR PSYCH ARTIST

In a tournament match you have an obligation to your opponent not to talk more than is necessary. Talking detracts from the quality of play, and breaks concentration. When you are faced with a talkative opponent, and he directs conversation to you, try to cut if off in a courteous manner. To reduce his temptation to converse, it is often best for you to towel off at the opposite net post.

There was one astonishing match I witnessed in which the players were not unethical but did not restrict their conversation to off-court remarks. In the late 1950s Gardnar Mulloy and Tony Vincent were playing in the final of the Coral Gables–University of Miami tournament, in Florida. On this clay surface the rallies were endless since the players were extremely steady and Mulloy surmised that going to the net that day meant annihilation. (Vincent preferred to remain in the back of his court against almost all opponents.) Mulloy, who was never short of bravado, decided, in the middle of a point in the arduous first set, to broach conversation. "Come on in and attack me, Vincent!" he said. Vincent replied, "*You* can come into the net if you want!" The crowd was startled with this breach of custom. The two were actually conversing with each other during the middle of the points. The umpire said nothing and took the viewpoint that since neither contestant objected, the dialogue should be allowed to continue. And it did, as the verbal exchange drifted to a subject beyond the realm of tennis. In between chatting, they played enough points for Vincent to push his way to victory, something he usually did not achieve against Mulloy. The Miami papers wrote up the match as the "talkathon." I had never seen a match like this before, and have not witnessed one since.

There are a few unethical players who will try to break concentration by making a calculated remark. Try to disregard this, but if the comments are upsetting, tell your opponent in no uncertain terms you would appreciate his keeping these comments to himself.

Speaking of psych artists, a number of years ago, there was a top-ten world-class Swedish player who had a reputation for attempting to derail opponents with a few carefully chosen words. He would try to gain an advantage on the opponent even before coming out of the locker room. The leader of the great Australian Davis Cup tennis team was so wary of the Swede's questionable tactics that he wisely ordered the team to stay away from him prior to their Davis Cup encounter. If Australia lost the series, the captain wanted it to be a result of Sweden's fine on-court play, and not any off-court remarks. Tennis conversation can be very interesting and satisfying, and should be conducted before a tournament match begins and after it ends.

THE DELIBERATELY BAD OR THE INCOMPETENT BALL-CALLER

Improper calling of balls creates by far the most problems on a tennis court. The importance of line calls can be underscored by the fact that just two or three incorrect calls can turn the tide of a match. It is important for a tennis player to have the ability to make close but fair calls. When a ball lands extremely near a line, and there is doubt as to whether it is in or out, the ball should be called good. (Nicholas Powell's Code, which was adopted in the rules of the United States Tennis Association, gives a lengthy rationale for this decision in favor of the opponent.)

If, however, you are giving your opponent the benefit of the doubt on balls he hits close to the line, and he is calling your marginal balls out, something must be done to rectify the situation. Otherwise, you might find yourself losing a match that you should have won. If you feel strongly that he is cheating on calls, you can simply walk up to the net and discuss it. It should be added that when players feel their opponents are honest in their calls, they usually tend to be honest when calling balls on their side of the net.

When an obviously bad call is made against you, first ask yourself, "Has my opponent played any of my *out* balls?" If he is making "two-way" mistakes that cost *him* points, and give him points as well, although this can be a little disconcerting, it is not such a serious threat. However, if all of his "mistakes" are costing *you* points, then you should take measures to protect yourself.

When an opponent makes a gross blunder in calling your ball out, you have every right to appeal to him. Simply say, "I thought that ball was good." There is a possibility you can persuade him to reverse his decision, or perhaps convince him to replay the point. Even if you lose the point, it is beneficial to question his call tactfully and put him on notice that you will not be pushed around in the match. Do not question his call on balls that you are unsure of, since this can upset him and disrupt the match.

If you are scheduled to oppose a notoriously bad caller or a poor sportsman (or even a big server), it is often advisable to request an umpire before the match. An umpire should be called during the middle of a match if you are constantly receiving bad calls, or if you are having difficulty making accurate calls.

One year I was playing a New England Tennis Association tournament in Westfield, Massachusetts, and I became the victim of some horrendous calls. (This happens very seldom.) I finally called for an umpire at the end of the first set, and what an umpire I got! I first asked the referee, William LeBreque, if he could dig up an official. Bill looked around for a few minutes and reported there was no one available. After asking some spectators if anyone would like to umpire the match, I finally came across a stranger who said he "did not have much experience," but he would "help out." As we were walking out toward the court, he casually mentioned he had refereed some "pick-up" basketball games. I was hesitant after hearing this attempt at documenting his ability to handle our match. However, since I was desperate for help, I thought *any* assistance would be better than none, so we continued to march out to the court. My suspicions of his qualifications were immediately verified as I noticed he did not assume the normal position at the net post. Instead, he stood on my side of the court near the service line as *I* served. I thought to myself, this is a new position for umpiring, but maybe he can do the job. I asked our just-found umpire if he was ready, and he replied that he was, so I served the ball to start the point. What followed was a classic in tennis officiating. He proceeded actually to *run* up and down the sidelines as the ball was being hit back and forth! When the ball finally landed wide of the court boundary lines, he threw up his arm with thumb high in the air and yelled, "Out!" I could not believe what I had just seen. I did not say anything, since *I* was responsible for bringing him out, and also figured that my opponent would blow his stack very shortly, anyway. He did just that within a minute or two, and after a long explanation, my adversary persuaded the guy to remain in one place. After what my opponent did to me with some of his bad calls, I rather enjoyed his being discomfited by my imported umpire. After the match, the umpire quickly admitted that he had never seen a tennis match refereed.

FOOT-FAULTER

If your opponent is hurting you on service by foot-faulting, you have a perfect right to ask him to cease this practice. If he continues to violate the rules, you may call for an umpire, or, under the new rule, you are authorized to call a foot fault yourself. If you tolerate foot-faulting, you are reinforcing an undesirable habit. In the vast majority of foot-fault cases, if the server will move away from the baseline about two to six inches, the problem will be solved. Naturally, you can offer this suggestion to your opponent.

QUICK OR SLOW SERVER

If the server walks unusually quickly to the serving position and serves, it is perfectly all right, as long as he is not gaining an advantage on you by doing so. However, if you believe his quick-serving manner has cost you points, then you should take action to prevent him from continuing to do this. You have a right not to be rushed (or stalled) by a server. If you feel the server is hurrying you, either accidentally or intentionally, you should slow down the tempo. This can best be done by holding the balls in your hand until you take the receiving position, and *then* returning them to the server. Also, you can look down to the ground for a couple of seconds just before he starts to serve. The rules state that the receiver must be ready to receive service before the serve can be delivered.

A valid question that officials should think more about is, how much time should a player be allowed in serving a ball? Although it is rare that this subject comes up in a match, there seems to be a need to establish a "ballpark" figure or time limit, to prevent any psyching. When a player makes a long delay as he is about to serve, knowingly or unknowingly, he can produce anxiety in some receivers. Although neither is called on it, there are a few players who would object to Jimmy Connors' or Brian Gottfried's bouncing a ball as many as seven or eight times before he serves. It seems that two or three bounces should suffice in making the server relax prior to commencing the point.

STALLER

A tennis match resembles a convoy in that it can go only as fast as its slowest member. When a player is tired, he cannot be blamed for moving at a slower pace. In hot weather, a player will also move more sluggishly than usual. We cannot fault a player who takes the allowable maximum of a full minute for changeovers. Players wearing glasses will have to wipe them regularly. Shoelaces will also occasionally need tying. Nevertheless, some matches reach the point where they are proceeding so slowly that play is almost not "continuous," as required by the rules.

One of your alternatives in dealing with a staller is to approach him diplomatically and ask him if he needs to take so much time to play. If this has no effect, you have the right to call for an umpire, whose very presence usually extracts at least a minimum standard of civilized court behavior. As a last resort, you can take even more time than the staller does at the changeover, and give him a taste of his own medicine.

INCORRIGIBLE OPPONENTS

There are some players whose immature behavior will probably never change. It is best you understand this, but you should never completely accept unethical conduct on a tennis court. Bad sportsmen in tennis invariably end up hurting themselves. Ilie Nastase, of Rumania, has created problems for himself by stalling and blabbing during matches. He has been heavily fined, and has found himself among hostile galleries. Tennis is too great a game to have it spoiled by offensive behavior, regardless of how "colorful" it may be.

ADDITIONAL REMARKS ON ETHICAL AND UNETHICAL BEHAVIOR

Following are some miscellaneous suggestions with regard to court conduct:

1. Aiming a groundstroke directly at a person from a relatively close range is proper if it is tactically advantageous, and if there is no intent to injure. If, by chance, you do hit someone, be sure to follow up by saying, "Are you okay?" or some such remark. In my opinion, directing an overhead smash at a person's feet or legs is proper, but certainly it is wrong to aim for the opponent's body. Be sure to understand that some rivals have the attitude that it is the receiving player's *total* responsibility to move out of the way of a ball by running or ducking. Some players who are in a vulnerable and defensive position turn their backs on the hitter for the sake of self-preservation.
2. Do not belittle an opponent's ability by carrying on a conversation with spectators during a match.
3. When you have hit a ball outside of your opponent's court, and he mistakingly continues to play it, call it out yourself if you are *sure* that this is the case. If you *think* your ball was out, but are not positive, do not say anything. Neal Freaser, the great Australian player, was also a champion in this regard. In a tough match in the French Championship he went so far as to give his opponent a very important point when he realized the linesman had erred. He did this on the following point by intentionally returning the service out of court.

The kinds of undesirable behavior mentioned in this chapter are, fortunately, rare. Tennis has an almost unequaled and distinguished tradition of honesty and propriety, and it is dependent upon us to preserve this heritage.

The subject of the next chapter, maintaining concentration, is a vital aspect of the game, and without it we cannot perform at anywhere near our potential.

Chapter 27

TACTICS TO DEVELOP CONCENTRATION

If two tennis players are of equal ability in stroke production and physical condition, the player with the best concentration will win every time. In an uphill fight, the resolute player will hang in mentally, long after the spasmodically attentive opponent has thrown in the towel of defeat.

WHAT IS CONCENTRATION?

Good concentration is total absorption in what you are doing. In tennis, this means alertness in anticipating your opponent's shots, and the ability to keep your eye on a moving target—the ball. It means watching and focusing on the seams of the ball as it is approaching. When you properly isolate the task of stroking the ball, you automatically block out extraneous thoughts. You do not think about the club where you are playing, the spectators watching you, the appearance and remarks of your opponent, or problems you might be facing off the court. Concentration should be a refreshing diversion from what might have been a tension-filled match. By centering your thoughts on one primary target, your body reacts with more authority. Concentration is synonymous with intelligent tennis, and in tennis, as well as other avenues of life, it produces positive results.

SIGNS OF CONCENTRATION, OR THE LACK OF IT

Concentration is involved in each stroke you produce, and it affects the whole match, from the first ball to the last. Hitting four or five unforced errors in a row is an obvious sign of a lapse of concentration. I try to use my return of service as a criterion in judging my concentration. Provided I am not going for winners or extremely low returns of service, I should rarely miss this shot. Continually losing track of the score can be a sign of diffused attention, although it does happen to all of us occasionally.

TECHNIQUES TO INDUCE AND IMPROVE CONCENTRATION

Since serious personal problems interfere with concentration, they must be largely solved before the player can reach the height of his athletic ability. Assuming a player is reasonably free from annoying or deep-seated problems, here are some techniques for improving concentration:

1. Periodically tell yourself and others, "I have good concentration," or, "My concentration is improving." This is a positive method of psyching yourself up.
2. Never play tennis without concentrating and stroking carefully. Concentrate even if you are having the most insignificant rally. Watch the ball carefully, and try hard to place the ball on the target you are aiming at. Take pride in your powers of concentration, especially when far behind in score. For example, if you have dropped eleven straight games and are obviously going to lose, try to offer resistance during that twelfth game.
3. Before the match begins, develop primary and secondary game plans (see Chapter 3). Among other benefits, this will help alleviate anxiety and doubt. Your concentration improves when you are firm in your intentions.
4. During the match warmup, watch the spin of the ball, and attempt to read the label. This technique induces a relaxed state of concentration.
5. Clear all balls lying on the ground that are either within the court boundaries or in your playing area, so that you do not lose concentration or injure yourself.
6. Avoid looking at the spectators except incidentally. Experienced tournament players rarely stare at the audience for prolonged periods. One of the few who got away with it was Ed Rubinoff, a Floridian, who was a soft-stroking left-handed net rusher. If he had possessed a serv-

ice to match his concentration, he would have been a champion.

7. Do not engage in conversation with your opponent or with the audience. If a passerby asks a question or makes a remark, you can respond courteously but briefly. When playing a loquacious opponent, it is often best to towel off at the opposite net post, so that court gossip will be preserved for the locker room. Whatever you do, refuse to become involved in someone's tennis problems during the middle of any match.

8. Since composure is an important prerequisite for concentration, attempt to maintain it. By acting calmly, and even by talking to yourself quietly, you will tend to remain in a relaxed state. Calmness on the court was epitomized by the great French player René Lacoste. Those, including Tilden, who had locked horns with this robot type of baseliner were in awe of his superlative powers of concentration. Hardly ever did "the Crocodile" lose control of himself, even when, as he put it, he "felt like making an outburst."

9. Forget past mistakes as well as winning shots, and concentrate on the present point and game. In this sense, have a very short memory and proceed with the task at hand.

10. Develop an intense desire to win specific points. Concentration will not be a problem when you are in pursuit of a point you desperately want to win.

Concentration is closely related to other mental aspects of the game. Controlling tension and developing confidence are very important topics that every player should fully understand, and they are the subjects of the next chapter.

Chapter **28**

TACTICS TO REDUCE TENSION AND BOLSTER CONFIDENCE

There is some overlap between overcoming nervousness and building confidence, and as these are interrelated factors, they have been combined in this chapter. In addition to aiding your game, building confidence should help make your tournaments and match play more enjoyable.

TENSION

Some tension in tournament or match play is inevitable, since substantial personal rewards can hinge on the outcome. You could be jockeying for a position on the ladder of a park or tennis club, aiming for a sectional or national ranking, or, in some tournaments, hoping to receive monetary rewards, depending on the outcome of a given match. In all of these cases, players have probably toiled like Trojans for extensive periods of time, and upon entering the important event, they risk the possibility of defeat. Such a loss can be shattering to the ego of the player who has not made a satisfactory adjustment. In the average tennis tournament, losing is the norm, and mental adjustments must be made to accommodate it. We must not forget that in a tournament with 128 players, there will be 127 losers. And half of the players do not even win a single match.

A certain amount of anxiety and respect for an opponent is desirable, since it will result in better match preparation, and may lessen the tendency to let up in a match. Although a slight amount of nervousness can keep the adrenaline active, excessive worry can have a paralyzing effect.

Most tournament competitors at one time or another have played poor matches because of uncontrolled tension. I recall such a match in 1961 when Australian Roy Emerson was scheduled to play the Indian touch artist Ramanthan Krishnan. It was a late-round singles match at the prestigious Wimbledon tournament. Here, practically all the players become apprehensive, since world rankings are at stake. In this world-famous tournament, which is conducted with precision, the players must be ready to walk on the court immediately after the preceding match is completed. A very lengthy contest occurred just prior to the Emerson-Krishnan event, and they were kept waiting unduly long in the locker room. When their turn finally came, and the warmup began, Roy noticed he had lost feeling for the grip and racket head. Emerson felt no better after the match began. He played poorly and lost (not to imply that Krishnan did not play well that day). However, even Krishnan would probably acknowledge that Roy did not play up to par in that encounter. Nervous performances marked much of Emerson's early tournament career. As he matured as a player, he conquered the problem of excessive tension, and became one of the toughest pressure players in history. During his career he lost only one of numerous Davis Cup challenge-round singles matches, and this was after the victory (over Spain) had already been decided. In addition to his outstanding playing ability, Roy Emerson is noted for his superb sportsmanship. He never offered excuses for a loss, and always extolled the play of his opponent.

It is very normal for young tennis players to have "cases of nerves" and then later to overcome them with more experience and tournament play. When players do not outgrow this tournament-nervousness stage, it is often the sign of deep-seated problems, and these individuals usually drop out of tournament tennis. Such was the case of a talented NCAA champion and Davis Cup player who was seen in recent years wandering aimlessly in parking lots in Beverly Hills, California. (He used to whistle throughout our practice matches.)

CONFIDENCE

Much has been written on the subject of confidence, and much of it has been misleading. Make no mistake about it—*confidence is not the cause of winning tennis but the result of winning tennis.* You cannot have confidence unless you have a sound game. There is no substitute for ball control and deeply grooved strokes achieved through diligent effort. You must first lay a firm foundation of solid strokes before you can construct the framework of confidence.

There are two varieties of confidence. One is based upon reality, and is responsible for an unshakable mental attitude. When you *know* what your strokes can and cannot do, you can be justifiably confident. The second type of confidence is abstract, unrealistic, and can result in disillusionment and frustration. The latter type is more accurately described as overconfidence.

I witnessed a vivid example of this latter "fool's gold" type of confidence a number of years ago in an international tournament in Aix-en-Provence, France. A reasonably talented American tennis player, who also had professional dancing ability, was playing a Czech Davis Cup player. During the first set, the American had a hot hand, executing delicate touch volleys, drop shots, and solid serves. The American was serving and leading five games to three. An error by the Czech and two fine volleys by the American gave him a 40–0 lead in the ninth game. At this point, the American stopped play, turned to the crowd, and with a big grin made the following statement: "I have been ground into hamburger on a tennis court long enough in my life, and this time it is *my* turn to make chopped meat out of somebody else!" He turned to his opponent and said, "This time you're the hamburger!" The crowd looked on in stunned silence. Then they started to giggle and react excitedly. They seemed to enjoy this temporary detour from the staid environment of the normal tennis match. The fans thought, What incredible confidence this relatively unknown American is displaying in making his seasoned international opponent look like a beginner. The brazen American was not finished with his presumptuous remarks. He swaggered up to the service line and yelled even more boastfully, "Five-three, forty-love, serving for the set!" The Czech glared at his cock-sure opponent, who then served and cleanly volleyed the ball away to win the first set. By now the Czech was so angry he was cursing under his breath. From the look on his face the match had taken on gigantic dimensions, and victory seemed to be as important as a win

over the Russian Davis Cup team. Play started in the second set, and the Czech won the next *twelve* games in a row to win the match. The American had disturbed a giant, one who was out of his class. Although the American had legitimately won a set, the tennis-playing dancer's skill was far below that of the Czech Davis Cupper. Perhaps two or three years of intensive international play could have brought him up to a near-equal ability level; however, at this time, the difference in ability was irreconcilable. Wishful thinking or false confidence cannot win a match for you when facing someone two or three classes above you.

The kind of confidence you should seek is that which enables you to play your best during a match, considering your assets and limitations. If you have only a three-cylinder engine, and the maximum speed your car can go is twenty miles per hour, then you should not be content to limit yourself to fifteen miles per hour. If you have a super-eight motor, and have the proved talent to cruise at seventy miles per hour, then you should take intelligent moves to operate at that fast speed.

The following suggestions to help overcome tension and bolster confidence have been divided into two catagories: long-term tactics and day-of-the-match tactics.

LONG-TERM TACTICS

Surround yourself with positive and supportive friends. Family and friends can be helpful in minimizing tension and helping your game. An aspiring player can benefit from a parent, spouse, or supportive friend who reinforces specific behavior patterns or performance goals he is seeking. For example, a volatile nineteen-year-old might be told by a parent, "It was nice to see you so calm in that final set. You are gaining greater self-control all of the time." Or the wife of a player who knew he used his forehand too defensively could comment, "I enjoyed those two crosscourt forehands you knocked off for winners today."

Just as we are wise to gravitate toward supportive people, we should also shy away from unhealthy influences. There are a few caustic and uninformed folks who, if given the opportunity, will tell us what they think. For example, after a heart-breaking loss, they might remark that we must have played badly in the match, or they simply do not understand how so-and-so could ever beat us. These kind of remarks are not helpful. Constructive criticism is almost always beneficial to an aspiring player, but it will not do him any good to listen to a "Negative Nat" type of character. It is advisable to avoid these personalities, since they can turn you off from the game. Discuss your tennis game only with knowledgable individuals who are positive thinkers, and who have your welfare in mind. Criticism should be only of the constructive type. Children are lucky to have the kind of parents who encourage and support their tennis.

Learn correct grips and strokes, practice regularly, and keep fit. No item is more important than learning proper grips and strokes that will offer the most leverage and enable your racket strings to remain on the ball for the maximum amount of time. Then you must hit thousands upon thousands of balls, both while drilling on specific shots and while playing sets. You can also benefit from using a backboard to groove your strokes. Only when grips and strokes have been practiced for years and years will they stand up well in pressure-packed situations. As you work on your game, you should develop a solid defense that will be reliable in difficult matches.

Do some running, so that you can have the added confidence that your physical condition is equal or superior to that of your opponent. It gives you a secure feeling when you know that the longer a match lasts, the better off you are.

Uneasiness and apprehension are bound to accompany the player who enters a tournament when he is out of condition. Engaging in a tournament is much like entering a lecture hall to take a final exam. For the student who has not studied and prepared, it is a painful experience; whereas the testing period can almost be pleasurable for the person who has done his homework. Anxiety is minimized in a tournament when we know that all possible preparations have been made beforehand. We enter the event knowing that we are entitled to a good match.

Enter tournaments. When a player performs better in practice than in tournaments, it is a sign that he is nervous during the latter. To enable you to play as well in tournaments as you do in practice, you should enter as many tournaments as possible. You will gain the opportunity to play in diverse conditions, which will add to your experience and confidence. In addition, you will have the opportunity to talk with better players, and will hold them less in awe.

Develop steadiness. A player will always be apprehensive unless he has the ability to keep the ball in play when the pressure is greatest. Excessive tension

can cause a loss in precision. The player with overspin on service and groundstrokes has a much greater safety margin than the flat-hitting stylist. The flat server and groundstroker is more susceptible to "off days," since fine timing is necessary to make these shots accurately. Use a moderate amount of spin in your game and you will not be overly troubled by erratic strokes. You will then be confident in being able to play steady tennis.

Schedule tough competition most of the time. When you schedule mostly tough competition during your practice sessions, you are taking out insurance for your tournament matches. Try to play plenty of superior players in practice, so that you will have added confidence in a tournament match, knowing you have faced the very best in practice.

Still, you should periodically play someone a level or two below you, to help you appreciate your own tennis ability. (I know of two international-class tennis players who would periodically slip off the main circuit and head to smaller local tournaments for the purpose of building their confidence.)

Do not pretend to be better than you are and do not make predictions. A few players will put pressure on themselves by implying to others they are more skilled than they actually are. Although tournament players will try to psych themselves up by making statements such as "I feel I will hit well against him," they are very reluctant ever to make a flat forecast of victory.

As a college-tennis coach, I was once guilty of making such a "we will beat so-and-so" statement. We had some very good teams at CCNY, and one year there was an exceptional group. A few days before we were slated to take on the Manhattan College tennis team, a reporter from the campus newspaper asked about my feelings on the upcoming match. Usually, my replies were on the conservative side, such as, "We can't take St. John's lightly," or, "I don't know that much about Seton Hall, but they are probably tough." This time I allowed my gut feeling to intrude, and with a touch of theatrics I blurted out, "We'll make pussycats out of Manhattan's tennis team!" Since reporters relish such offerings, this appeared prominently in the next issue of the campus paper. Of course, I paid for this indescretion by having to sweat this match out more than usual. I would have been the laughingstock of the campus had we lost, but fortunately we did not. Remember—modesty and maturity reduce the pressure.

Do not make any type of a grip or stroke change

in the middle of the tournament season. The liabilities inherent in making any major changes during the tournament season (such as switching from an Eastern grip to the Continental grip, or changing your service motion) greatly outweigh the assets. If you strongly desire to alter your game, then defer tournament playing until you are positive that these alterations are firmly established. Otherwise, you will suffer the discouragement of shaky strokes that produce tension and a loss of confidence.

Certain mental exercises can be beneficial in reducing tension. You might find it helpful to try and visualize the match beforehand. Days or hours before the match begins, you can picture what the match will entail, from walking on the court to the playing of points. Imagine yourself hitting winning shots. The underlying theory behind this idea is that picturing the match situation beforehand might make you feel more at home when the actual event takes place. Mentally, you are accustomed to the surroundings, since you have been there, in thought, before.

Another technique that might ease tension is to imagine, when competing with a friend in practice, that you are playing a tough tournament match. You might say to yourself, just before hitting a second serve, "This is match point against me in the final of the National Championship, and I have to put this ball in play."

Some players who are overly anxious before tournament matches prefer to reconcile themselves to defeat before even walking on the court, as immunization against the shock of a possible loss.

Incorporate relaxation and diversion with serious training programs. It is necessary that you learn which activities produce the most pleasure and the least tension when you are not playing tennis. You will want to indulge yourself in these as a means of relaxation and diversion to complement your tennis-training program. Many tournament players make a point of removing themselves from the tennis environment and from tennis talk as soon as their practice or match is over. Relaxation, though beneficial at all levels of tennis, is essential for the tournament competitor. Parties, movies, concerts, card games—whatever brings you the most pleasure—must be balanced with your tennis regimen. Otherwise, your tennis growth might be stunted.

DAY-OF-THE-MATCH TACTICS

Relax beforehand. Although you might have had a hectic week, it is absolutely essential that you have ample relaxation on the day of the match.

Schedule a warmup. If you are prone to nervousness, be certain to take a lengthy warmup a few hours before the match begins. For some players, twenty or twenty-five minutes is sufficient, whereas others need an hour or so to work off nervous energy and gain racket touch. If an opponent or a court is unavailable, hitting on a backboard will suffice.

Adopt a "hitting balls is fun" approach. You can say to yourself, "It's a beautiful day for playing tennis, and I am going to enjoy this match." Think of what fun it will be to hit new balls back and forth over the net. One of Jimmy Connors' former coaches told me that his pupil had this attitude. Connors worked to develop the knack of going into matches looking forward to the opportunity to bash the ball. He also tried to cultivate the idea of enjoying the match even more when his opponent returned many balls and prolonged the rallies!

Do not listen to criticism from anyone just prior to, or during, a tournament.

If you are quite nervous as you walk on the court, work hard in the warmup. As soon as you feel your body is loose and warm, start vigorously to chase down balls that are almost beyond your reach. This tough limbering up will stand you in good stead when the match begins.

Watch the ball carefully during the warmup. By concentrating continuously from the first ball hit in the warmup, you will have less of a tendency to let your mind wander to the spectators or to other extraneous thoughts. When you focus your complete attention on the ball, your mind is less inclined to become bogged down with apprehension.

Be thoroughly familiar with the equipment you use. When you come out for a match using a racket for the first time, you are bound to have problems unless it is absolutely identical to your others. Also, break in your shoes, especially leather ones, before you use them in a tournament match.

Between points, walk slowly and breathe deeply. Taking a deep breath before you serve or return serve can be especially beneficial. You can even talk to yourself quietly to calm your nerves.

Aim for a high percentage of first serves in play. By getting a higher percentage of first serves in play, you prevent the tension that builds up when you begin to deliver your second service.

When behind in the match, do not give up. Do not feel that all is lost should you drop behind in the match, since some players have difficulty maintaining a lead or winning. There are a number of skillful players who cannot hit freely and offensively when they get close to victory. Be ready to seize this opportunity.

Do not berate yourself during the match. Do not tear your own game down by making self-condemnations, such as, "I am lousy—my backhand is no good," etc. You will not improve confidence or your self-image this way.

Use some positive self-psyching. If you are the underdog, but are capable of upsetting your opponent on a good day, you can think about whispering the following statements to yourself: "I have practiced long and hard enough, and now I deserve to win this match"; "I am going to play well today because I have good concentration powers and I am relaxed"; "I am going to win today because my opponent feels I am going to win."

Do not have hostile feelings toward your opponent. When you go to the court with a hostile attitude, you are bound to enjoy the match less, and will be more nervous than you ordinarily would. Be courteous.

If you lose the match, your opponent deserves the victory. Give your opponent full credit for the victory, since he played well, or at least better, and do not fret or be overly concerned if you do not win the match. Keep a positive attitude, and, as quickly as you can, write down your analysis of the match so that when you meet him again, you will be better prepared to cope with his style of game.

True confidence involves a thorough knowledge of one's own game as well as an understanding of an opponent's capabilities. I will conclude this chapter with a story that typifies the nature of genuine confidence.

William Alvarez, an international-class player from Colombia, was a player who had realistic confidence. He was capable of winning everything possible, given the constraints of his talent. Alvarez was average in height, with stocky legs. He was shrewd, and had a thorough understanding of how to cope with certain kinds of games. This insight was achieved through many years of tennis-tournament wars. Alvarez enjoyed the tennis court as a stage, and would often place himself in the center of dramatic and controversial spectacles. One time we were in a tournament at the Carlton Hotel, in Cannes, France. While we were in the middle of a routine practice session, he asked me if I knew whom he was scheduled to play in the next round. I told him I had not noticed his draw, and he replied that he was playing Jaime Pinto-Bravo, of Chile. My comment was, "It's going to be a tough match." It seemed like a rational statement to make, since Pinto-Bravo's record was almost equal to that of Alvarez; each had many excellent wins to his credit. In a shrill voice, almost gloating, Alvarez said, "He has no chance; I will beat him six-one six-one, or six-one six-two!" "What gives you that kind of confidence?" I asked. "No way he can hurt me," said William. The hour of the match approached, and my curiosity compelled me to make a special trip to the courts to observe this encounter. Alvarez saw me take a seat, and immediately came over and made just one statement: "Remember what I said!" They finished the warmup and started play. The first game lasted fifteen minutes, and the ball must have gone back and forth over the net 300 times. Alvarez won the first game. Sweating profusely, he took a couple of swigs of orange soda from a quart bottle that he always had with him. They then started the second game, and Alvarez also won this one after about 100 exchanges. The rallies became shorter and shorter as Pinto-Bravo's resistance was broken down. Alvarez nodded to me a time or two with an I-told-you-so look. He was reveling in the expression of disbelief reflected on the faces of late-arriving spectators when the announcement of the one-sided score was made. Finally, the roof fell in completely on the Chilean. Alvarez beat him as badly as he had predicted. Looking back over the years at these two outstanding players, one realizes that there was a very fine but definite difference in ability when they played against each other. Alvarez had the experience of knowing that he was just a hair more consistent from the baseline than his fellow South American, and since Pinto-Bravo could not hurt him by attacking, Alvarez had the confidence of knowing that victory was his, even before walking on the court.

An ample amount of confidence and an absence of excessive tension are attributes well within the grasp of most players. But these are only a part of the proper and positive attitude that we should strive to develop when playing the game of tennis.

Chapter 29

DEVELOPING THE PROP-ER ATTITUDE FOR TEN-NIS

We must never lose sight of the fact that for the vast majority of players, tennis is but a game. Though it is played with serious intent, for most participants it is primarily a source of recreation that provides healthy exercise, relaxation, and friendships. These pleasures are not dependent upon winning. We have reached the ultimate in tennis maturity when we are able to treat winning and losing with equal consideration. For some players, the pleasure in the game is simply to be graceful, and to try to hit the ball cleanly in the center of the racket strings and over the net. This attitude is fine for them. For others, tennis offers the opportunity of a constant challenge to perfect a complex athletic skill.

TENNIS AND MENTAL HEALTH

By selecting tennis as one of the two sports he would include in his utopian society, B. F. Skinner, the noted Behaviorist, writing in *Walden Two*, placed great psychological value on the sport. Tennis has a very positive effect on one's mental health. We gain self-esteem and self-confidence through the mastery of this complex skill. It is a means of recognition, regardless of where we stand in the pecking order of ability. We might make a nice shot or play a good game, and people will notice this and congratulate us for it. Through tennis, children can develop tolerance, as can adults. Although mastery of the game can be trying, tennis is basically a healthy activity.

REWARDS IN TENNIS

As most of us know, developing a tennis game can be a very satisfying and beneficial experience. The young and elderly can enjoy the game together, and it is truly a family sport. For me it is a pleasure to hit with my wife, who is not a tournament player. Unlike many other physical activities, tennis can be pursued for a lifetime. You can almost always find one person to play with. No competitive sport requires fewer participants (a minimum of two for singles, and a maximum of four for doubles), yet offers as many attainable goals and performance levels.

Attainable goals and performance levels. There are goals to be reached in comparing your game with others' games. Players who have limited experience receive satisfaction by attaining better scores against their friends. The more skillful player can rise to a higher position within his peer group, or even advance to the next category. Some categories of players are: a good park or club player, a park or club champion, a college-varsity player, a ranking state player, a sectionally ranked player, and a nationally ranked player.

There are tournaments and cup matches organized according to age and sex that offer rankings and trophies. There are junior tournaments for girls and boys under 12, 14, 16, 18, and 21 years of age; men's and women's tournaments for all players; junior veterans' tournaments for men over 35; senior competition for women over 40; and veterans' competition for men over 45, 50, 55, 60, 65, 70, 75, and even 80 years of age.

Financial rewards. For the exceptionally talented player there also can be monetary rewards. Young men and women are awarded college tennis scholarships. Teaching professionals receive excellent compensation, as do playing professionals. However, only a handful of players in the world are in the latter category and make a great deal of money. For some circuit players, prize money is eaten up by heavy traveling expenses. Considering the incredibly long apprenticeship necessary to compete on this high level, tennis-playing professionals certainly deserve whatever tangible rewards they receive.

TENNIS ETHICS

Tennis demands a high standard of behavior. We must conduct ourselves as ladies and gentlemen or, in the broader sense, we will be very unsuccessful in tennis. We should preserve the fine tradition of ordinary politeness such as the handshake and saying please and thank you. Propriety and courtesy are the expected modes of behavior and should be carefully adhered to.

As spectators, we correctly learn to appreciate the good shot with a responsive clap, but should refrain from applauding the unforced error.

ATTITUDE TOWARD YOUR OPPONENT (PARTNER)

Throughout this book I have referred to the person on the opposite side of the net as the "opponent." This term was simply used for clarification. Since you need each other in order to have a game, a more appropriate term to use is "partner."

Accept the inevitable fact that in most matches your opponent will receive a few lucky breaks. He is going to hit a couple of let-cord (net-tape) winners, and he will probably hit a few shots that barely touch the outsides of your lines.

Courtesy. You owe your partner the common courtesy of being on time for your practice or tournament match, and of offering to split the cost of the balls. If he is a member of a club, and you are his guest, you should always supply the balls, since he has to pay a guest fee. You should not place your relationship under any undue strain by offering to bet money on the outcome of the match. Also, your partner deserves the right to play the match without having to contend with remarks designed to upset his game. Also, he deserves to be acknowledged for making an outstanding shot.

Resist opponent. Although you should have positive attitudes toward your partner, make no mistake about it—you should do your best to try to win the match. You should attempt to give him the hardest and most frustrating time possible in having to cope with your shots, and you want to make yourself a problem in his eyes by returning as many of his balls as possible. If you are winning, you should try to get him off the court as quickly as you can. If you are losing, you want him to sweat out the victory in the most laborious manner. You want him to respect your tennis game and your personal tenacity, and the only method of doing this is to make him earn his points. You should attempt to give him as few outright gifts (errors) as possible.

WHEN THE MATCH ENDS

After the match is over, if you have lost, try not to make any excuses to your partner. Assume a "more power to him" attitude regarding his deserved victory. In the postmatch remarks, emphasize his good playing and not your poor play, if such was the case. Be assured of the fact that if he beats you, he is better, at least on that day. Learning to be a gracious loser usually takes a little more time than learning to be a gracious winner. If you are fortunate enough to win, take a private moment to be proud, and savor the victory.

Chapter 30

GUIDELINES FOR INTEL-LIGENT TENNIS PLAY

LEARN CONSISTENCY FIRST; THEN STRIVE FOR POWER WITH CONSISTENCY

Beginners should swing slowly and stroke safely. In the early stages of tennis development, stroke slowly or with medium speed. In this embryonic period do not use excessive racket speed, since timing a very hard stroke is too difficult for your level of play. Swinging the racket faster than you are capable will result in frustration caused by a rash of errors. When a player hits more than three or four feet over the baseline or errs into the bottom half of the net, he is probably overhitting. Equally risky is trying to place balls too close to lines or corners, or clearing the net by too narrow a margin *(Fig. 30.1).*

Fig. 30.1 Beginners, do not skim the net. Use a safe (high) trajectory over the net when opponent is in the backcourt. A high ball also produces greater depth.

By overhitting, you could end up losing when you could have been victorious. Winning matches that we know we should win brings satisfaction, and tends to motivate us to play more tennis. As psychologists often say, "Behavior that is rewarded is repeated." Consistent losers tend to drift to other pastimes.

Remember, regardless of your playing ability, maintain ball control *(Fig. 30.2)*. Bobby Riggs, who was one of the greatest players ever, often said, "Play airtight tennis."

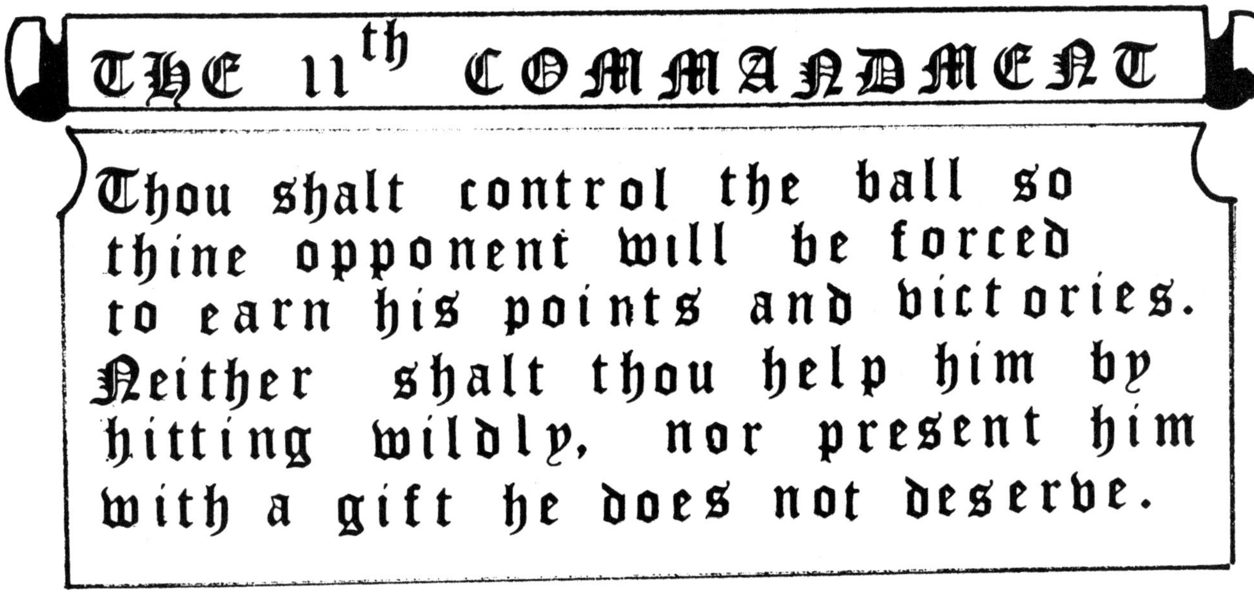

THE 11th COMMANDMENT

Thou shalt control the ball so thine opponent will be forced to earn his points and victories. Neither shalt thou help him by hitting wildly, nor present him with a gift he does not deserve.

Fig. 30.2 The Eleventh Commandment.

Top tennis requires power. In order to dent the armor of most tournament players, power must be added to control. Soft balls will usually not extract errors from top players, since timing slow balls is less of a problem for them than timing fast ones. There is not one outstanding professional touring player in the world today who does not hit the ball with very good pace. Do not allow anyone to convince you that two of the circuit's so called "softer hitters," Harold Solomon and his doubles partner, Eddie Dibbs, do not usually hit hard groundstrokes. Yes, Solomon hits an occasional soft "moon ball," but the pace on his groundstrokes is considerable when compared with that of Class "C," "B," and even "A"* tennis players. Every international-class player has at least one powerful shot that he can execute at will. Try to develop one or two shots that are going to score against anyone, and whose success is not dependent upon the opponent's error.

How do you learn to hit a hard ball? We develop pace through proper ball timing, using correct grips and strokes, applying maximum leverage, and keeping the racket strings on the ball for as long a period as possible. Thousands upon thousands of balls must be hit with correct form. However, even with proper stroking, a deliberate attempt must be made to acquire

*In certain parts of the world, tournaments and players are organized into categories such as Novice (lowest level), Class C, B, and A. Southern California has such a system. France has literally hundreds of players ranked according to ability.

pace. Periodically, say to yourself, "I am going to hit ten percent harder today than I usually do."

Those who play only on weekends will probably never be able to hit accurately with great ball speed, since their timing will never be fully developed. Others who have stroke weaknesses will also be limited to slower and perhaps shorter swings. Those of you who are in these categories should not be dismayed. You might have as much fun with your tennis game as Jimmy Connors does with his! Enjoyment of tennis and a person's level of play do not necessarily go hand in hand.

A tennis journey on railroad tracks. As you practice and play to improve your tennis game, think of yourself proceeding on a journey along railroad tracks. Imagine one of the rails as being control and consistency, and the other as being power and pace. Always stay in the middle of the tracks, between these two guideposts *(Fig. 30.3)*. Sometimes you will venture too far toward the control track and play too carefully; other times you will overhit a little bit. Most players should stay closer to the control track.

Fig. 30.3 Seek controlled power. Stay between the control and the power track as you proceed on your journey toward tennis improvement.

Try to control points. If your goal is to become very good, and you have the time available, plus fine strokes and athletic ability, think about controlling points as you develop your game. By that I mean *you* take the chances by producing the winning shot and by keeping your opponent on the move. This will help guarantee that you do not become too defensive as you are building your tennis game.

Making the first offensive shot. The logical method of gaining control of points is to take the initiative and make the first offensive shot of the point. Some players do this by serving aggressively; others, with an offensive return of service. In an exchange, when you place a ball deep and hard in the opponent's corner, he is forced to move to retrieve the ball, and it becomes difficult for him to return an offensive shot. In this case, the opponent simply tries to return your ball. Thus, you are able to follow up with another aggressive shot, keeping him on the defensive. Being the first person to take the offensive is the psychological equivalent of drawing "first blood" in a battle.

FROM THE BEGINNING OF YOUR TENNIS CAREER, HAVE A THOROUGH UNDERSTANDING OF WHAT YOU CAN AND CANNOT DO WITH EACH OF YOUR STROKES.

In order to be tactically efficient, you must know which of your shots is the most consistent. For example, is your backhand-topspin drive more accurate aimed down the line or crosscourt? Can this backhand shot be hit with great speed, or only moderately fast? Can the ball be effectively taken early (while it is rising from the ground), or must it be taken at its peak or on the downward flight? How close to the net can you consistently hit your passing shots? You must know what the odds or percentages are when using one shot instead of another (e.g., your forehand lob versus your forehand passing shot).

Use only proved and effective strokes and strategies in a match. The lack of a particular shot means you cannot utilize a certain tactic. If you do not have an accurate drop shot, you cannot use it in a match. If you are unable to bludgeon a serve, forget about serving and volleying against a good groundstroker on clay. If you cannot execute an overhead smash or volley, you must not come to the net. If you have not learned to hit the ball on the rise, you must forget about hitting passing shots off deep volleys while standing inside your baseline. One of the best

ways to determine what you can and cannot do on a tennis court (as well as to learn the shots themselves) is to engage in a wide variety of drills.

BE AWARE THAT A BALL LOSES APPROXIMATELY FIFTY PERCENT OF ITS SPEED AFTER BOUNCING

The above-stated fact is based on a principle called the "coefficient of restitution." Applied to tennis, it means that you receive balls at a much faster rate of speed when you volley than when you hit groundstrokes *(Fig. 30.4).* The volley backswing, of course, must be shorter, since there is little time available for preparation.

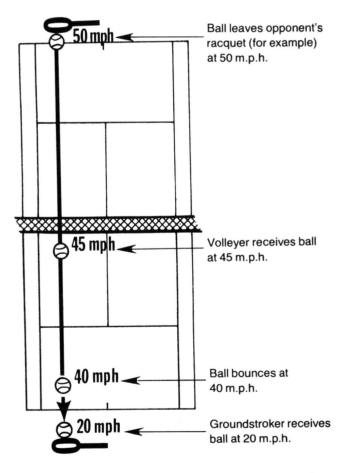

Fig. 30.4 The volleyer receives balls at a faster rate of speed than the groundstroker.

Also, you must realize that hitting a deep ground-stroke or volley to your opponent's baseline means it reaches him much faster than one hit equally hard but that bounces shorter, near the service line. This is one of the many advantages of hitting with good depth.

In addition, you should be aware that except for the high defensive lob, a ball loses considerable speed as it travels through the air, even before it hits the ground. A big 140-mph serve hit by Colin Dibley or Mike Sangster is not moving anywhere near that speed as it crosses the net. (Incidentally, a defensive lob should be hit as high as possible, since the higher the ball rises, the faster it descends.)

CONSTANT STROKE ADJUSTMENT IS NECESSARY TO ZERO IN ON TARGETS (Fig. 30.5)

This is especially important in the beginning stages of tennis. If you are trying to place the ball deep, but it is falling short in the court, program yourself by saying, "I will clear the net by four or five feet and keep the ball within the opponent's baseline. Under no circumstances, when he is in the back of the court, will I lower the trajectory of the ball so that it falls short or goes into the net."

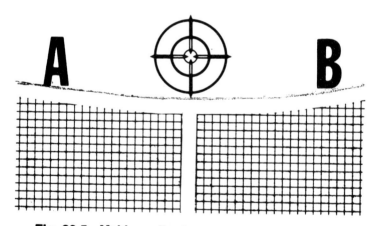

Fig. 30.5 Making adjustments to zero in on tennis target.
A. Making left-right adjustments.
1. If you are aiming at the target, but are hitting area A, adjust by aiming at area B.
2. If you are aiming at the target, but are hitting area B, adjust by aiming at area A.

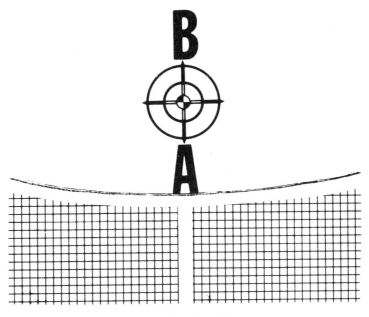

B. Making up-down adjustments.
1.   If you are aiming at the target, but are hitting level A, adjust by aiming at level B.
2.   If you are aiming at the target, but are hitting level B, adjust by aiming at level A.

Consider yourself an artilleryman who is constantly adjusting the direction of his cannon until he guides the shell to the proper target. If you misdirect your shells, you are certainly going to adjust the angle of your barrel in order to find the proper range. Similarly, you should adjust the trajectory of your shots.

DO NOT BECOME OVERLY ANXIOUS TO END A RALLY

Develop patience and a tough mental attitude regarding defense, which is so necessary, especially on clay. Say to yourself, "I will bide my time until I get the right ball to attack." If you do not have a good net game, and therefore cannot attack, simply say to yourself, "I will grind him down physically and mentally from the back of the court."

By extending rallies you can often force equally steady players to take risks and to try low-percentage shots that will cost them dearly. In order to execute this plan successfully, there is only one requirement besides steadiness: your physical condition must be equal or superior to your opponent's.

Extending rallies is especially worthwhile early in a match, or until you develop good timing of the opponent's shots. Much greater precision is necessary for offensive shots than for those made defensively, from the back of the court, with little thought toward ending the point.

WHEN MOVING TOWARD THE BALL, DECIDE QUICKLY AND FIRMLY ON THE SHOT YOU ARE GOING TO HIT

Lack of decisiveness in determining the type of stroke to be used, pace on the ball, and target to be aimed at can be costly. A player should say to himself, for example, that he will stroke a backhand slice, deep and crosscourt, with good pace. Planning specific patterns beforehand can be helpful, so that there will be less chance of stroking indecisively. You might say, for example, "I will hit my forehand groundstrokes crosscourt with topspin, and use the forehand slice down the line. On all backhands, with my opponent in the back of his court, I will slice, but on all backhand passing shots, with my opponent at the net, I will take the ball early and will use overspin. I will hit all overheads toward his backhand side unless I can get a clean winner on his forehand side," etc. The stronger and firmer the will of a player regarding the objectives of each stroke, the greater the chance of success.

USUALLY, AIM YOUR GROUNDSTROKES, VOLLEYS, AND OVERHEADS TOWARD THE OPEN COURT, AND EXPECT YOUR OPPONENT TO DO THE SAME

Your basic objective is to extract the error from the opponent while minimizing your own chances of erring. The most effective method of drawing an opponent's error is to make him hit shots while on the run, instead of allowing him to be poised at ball contact. When a tennis player is forced to hit while moving (especially sideways or away from the net), he will lose both precision and power. He is more likely to stroke short or mishit and allow you to attack him successfully. He will also become fatigued more quickly when moving than when hitting from the center of his baseline.

To force him to move, aim the ball to one sideline, then to the opposite sideline, then back to the first sideline. You can also "long-short" him, by stroking deep into one of his baseline corners, then hitting short, near the net, on the other side. If you have the stroking ability to hit near the sidelines, you can probably attack him on the second or third ball. Also, when you keep your opponent on the run, you are not usually vulnerable to an attack from him.

Once you get your opponent on the run, you can keep him off balance by using another ploy: hitting the ball back to the corner he returned it from, or "hitting behind" him *(Fig. 30.6)*. The main disadvantage of this tactic, as compared with hitting toward the open court, is that it is not as physically tiring to the opponent. When a player is "wrong-footed," he might have to take only three or four steps, whereas if he is forced to move to the open court, he might have to sprint twice or three times that distance.

Fig. 30.6 Wrong-footing the opponent. Directing your shot to the same corner opponent has returned the ball from.

When your opponent has *you* on the move and maneuvers you out of the center of the court, in most cases he will aim his next shot toward the part of the court that is unoccupied. This is his best opportunity for an outright winner. If you are a considerable distance off one side of the court, anticipate your opponent's ball by moving to the opposite side, even before he strokes, in order to retrieve his shot.

DO NOT USE ANY MORE STROKING POWER THAN IS NECESSARY TO ACCOMPLISH YOUR OBJECTIVE

If you have maneuvered your singles opponent to the side of the court in the doubles alley, and have a short, easy volley or an overhead to make, do not blast the ball with full power or aim too near the lines. A medium-paced ball landing farther from the sidelines is safer and will still produce an outright winner. In other words, use a fly swatter, not an elephant gun, to kill a fly. Always be aware that the greater the power used, the greater the chance of error.

LEARN WHEN TO HIT THE BALL HARD AND WHEN TO TAKE A RISK

Hitting with pronounced power to make a winning shot should be done with discretion. It is foolish to go for broke with a screaming drive to a corner from far behind your baseline when the opponent is in good position in the back of his court *(Fig. 30.7)*. A smart opponent would enjoy receiving such a shot, because he would have ample time to move to and return the ball.

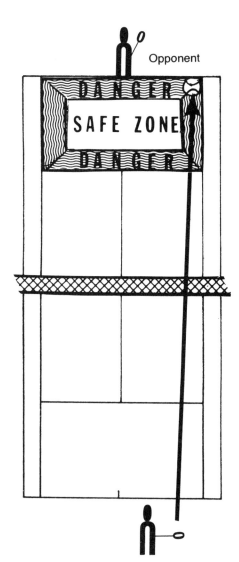

Fig. 30.7 Poor risk. With opponent in good position, and you far behind your baseline, do not attempt a very hard drive to a corner. Direct the ball to the safe zone.

Since there is danger in attempting a very hard shot, do it mainly in the following situations: when you can end the point on that shot or the next one; when your opponent is lodged at the net and you have been forced outside of the court boundaries and are running. In the latter situation, you can attempt a one-chance-in-five winner by blasting the ball, since hitting a shot at normal speed might award you the point in only one of twenty cases *(Fig. 30.8)*. You might also try hitting with great pace when you cannot hurt your opponent in any other manner, and are not winning any games employing normal tactics.

Fig. 30.8 Good risk. When badly out of position and on the run, attempt an outright winning shot, past the net man.

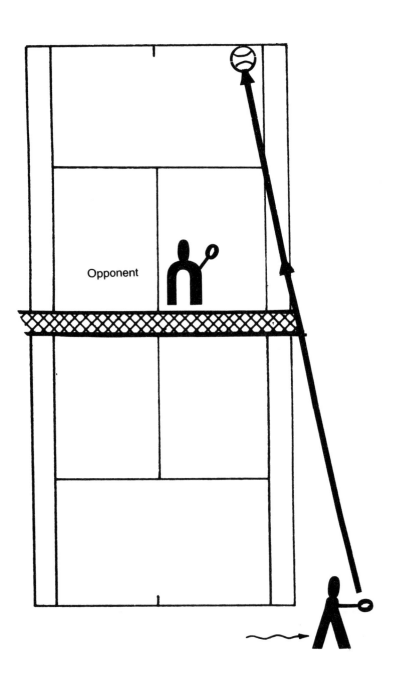

Opponent

ANALYZE THE TYPES OF SHOTS AND TACTICAL PLAYS THAT ARE GIVING BOTH YOU AND YOUR OPPONENT A HIGH PERCENTAGE OF WINNING POINTS

Your mind should be like a computer in analyzing the effect of your shots in a match. Alertness is necessary in giving you the feedback, for example, that your loop to an opponent's backhand is extracting a ten-percent error rate, whereas the same stroke to his forehand is resulting in a twenty-percent error rate. Make a strong mental note to yourself after every error he makes by answering the question, "What kind of a shot did I just give him?" A smart tennis player is acutely aware of probabilities.

Conversely, diagnose his winning or effective shots, and take remedies to minimize these. Let us say, for example, that your opponent is putting ball after ball away with his volley, especially on the forehand side. As a remedy, you can guide your groundstrokes deeper and harder, making his sojourns to the net more difficult. Or, you can give him more lobs and backhand volleys so that you will not be feeding balls directly into his strength. You can watch and ascertain if his forehand volleys are being aimed into a certain area of your court, and start moving in that direction as he is hitting the ball.

One-word solutions to problems. In buttressing your defense against an opponent's attack, you will discover that repeating one-word solutions to yourself can be helpful in solving a dilemma. "Deeper," "harder," "softer," and "lower" are succinct and easy-to-repeat instructions that can often turn a match in your favor.

Identical tactics against the same opponent will not always be successful. When analyzing what is occurring in a given match, you should not confuse data from other matches against the same opponent with the results of this encounter. Conditions, even against the same opponent, can vary considerably from match to match. Speed of the court, weight and condition of the balls, temperature, and momentum can vary so much that a shot that works well against your opponent one week will not be a winner against him the next.

For example, a number of years ago I was able to win a clay-court match at the last minute against a steady baseliner by suddenly coming to the net on every ball. A couple of weeks later I went into a match with the same fellow feeling confident that the net attack would work well for me again. It did not, and I was easily passed on identical courts! I was almost down the tubes before convincing myself that the exact strategy that had worked so well previously was the worst possible tactic to use *that* day. Perhaps my volleys lacked their normal sting, or maybe he was keeping his eyes closer to the ball while hitting passing shots. My new tactic was to remain, most of the time, in the back of the court, and to come to the net only when I had maneuvered him completely out of position.

In short, do not cling to any plan or preconceived notion if it is not paying off during a match.

THINK IN TERMS OF MATCHING YOUR STRENGTHS AND WEAKNESSES AGAINST THOSE OF YOUR OPPONENT

Directing your strength against the opponent's weakness. The ideal tactic is for you to pit your strengths against your opponent's weakness. For example, if you have an excellent serve to the backhand side, and your opponent happens to have a weak backhand, you have an established advantage. Or, if you have a net-rushing game and your opponent's passing shots are not strong, you can exploit this continually. If you can execute a great lob and your opponent has a weak overhead, you might have another advantage.

Your strengths versus your opponent's strengths. Suppose your strength happens to collide head on with his strength. For example, if your excellent serve to his backhand is matched by a very strong backhand, your net-rushing game is equalized by his fine passing shots, and your precise lob can be answered by his outstanding overhead—what do you do then? First of all, you must ascertain who will be slightly better off when a collision of your strengths occurs. Such a confrontation of force took place at Wimbledon when Jack Kramer played his renowned down-the-line sidespin forehand into Jarslov Drobny's incredible left-handed forehand. Kramer got burned by forcing this play on the Czech.

The great Bill Tilden, who had an inclination for the dramatic, claimed he would often disregard an opponent's weakness, and would intentionally direct an attack against his strength in order to break him down completely! This is fine for a Tilden or a Don Budge, but for the rest of us it is masochistic folly, and should be done only if we are losing points by hammering at his weakness.

Matching your weakness against your opponent's weakness. If it is not possible to match your strength against your opponent's weakness, and it is not advisable to pit your best stroke against his best stroke, then you should try your weakest stroke or game against his weakest.

Directing every ball to opponent's weakness. If the opponent has a glaring weakness, it might be best to forget about your own strengths and weaknesses and to direct every ball to his weak stroke. This will cause you to do more running, but it will almost certainly extract more errors. This tactic can break down an opponent psychologically.

UNDERSTAND THE MEANING OF PRESSURE AND HOW IT CAN HELP YOU WIN

The terms "pressure" and "offensive game" are often synonymous. The application of pressure ordinarily means attacking an opponent, and usually involves forecourt play. It means allowing the opponent less time to stroke a ball, by hitting the ball harder, or earlier. For example, by your coming to the net behind a good approach shot, the opponent at his baseline is allowed a smaller target and is forced to take chances by skimming the net or stroking a precise lob. He is often distracted and takes his eye off the ball. Applying pressure is risky and requires advanced serving, approach-shot, and net skills.

If you, like most players, cannot attack with accuracy over the length of an entire match, you are far better off playing steady and controlled tennis, keeping the ball in play.

CLOSING WORDS

In developing your tactics, perceive the tennis ball as a globe, and yourself as a pioneer setting out to conquer unexplored territory—the world of delicate angles, tantalizing spins, and penetrating volleys—with the racket as your means of transportation. Most of all, have fun on your journey. Tennis is a lifetime adventure.

GLOSSARY

These are the author's definitions of terms. To learn the specific names of the tennis-court areas and lines, refer to the diagram on page 150.

Descriptions of terms used in this book are explained from a right-hander's position.

Ad court. The left service court, or the service box on your left side, on your side of the net. The term *ad court* is derived from the score, meaning one of the players has the advantage (*ad*) in score when a point is started in this court; the score will always be odd.

All-court game. The ability to execute sound strokes from any part of the court, without any particular stroke weakness.

Angled volley or shot. A stroked ball which draws an opponent beyond the sideline of the court. The best angled shots are directed crosscourt, and made from as close to the net as possible.

Anticipation. Moving at the earliest possible moment in the direction the opponent will aim the ball. Good anticipation means less rushing and more accuracy in stroking.

Approach shot. An offensive groundstroke that is followed to net. A player usually approaches the net, or hits an approach shot, off an opponent's short, slow ball.

Automatic volley. Angling both backhand and forehand volleys crosscourt and short.

Backboard. A smooth wall that is used to stroke tennis balls against. The ball rebounds from the backboard with enough power and consistency to enable a person to maintain a rally.

Backcourt. The area between the service line and baseline where most advanced volleys and groundstrokes should land.

Backspin. *See* **Underspin.**

Backswing. Moving the racket in a backward direction to prepare for its forward movement. It is the first part of a stroke or serve, and is followed by the forward swing.

Baseliner or baseline player. A player who hits the vast majority of his shots as groundstrokes, instead of volleys. Most of his balls are hit from just behind the baseline.

Change of pace. Stroking the ball at different speeds in order to upset the timing of an opponent.

Concentration. The ability to block out extraneous thoughts to achieve a high level of tennis performance.

Controlling points. Placing the opponent on the defensive; thus, most points are decided by your winning shot or error.

Crosscourt. A ball directed diagonally across the court, not parallel with the sidelines. For example, right-handers hitting forehands to each other would be rallying toward each other's corners in a crosscourt manner.

Depth. The quality of serving the ball just inside the opponent's service line, or hitting it between the service line and the baseline during play. In top tournament tennis *good depth* means hitting the ball no farther than nine or ten feet from the opponent's baseline.

Deuce court. The right service court, or the service box on your right, on your side of the net. The term *deuce court* is derived from the score, meaning the total number of points played in the game is always even when a point is started in this court.

Dink. A low, soft ball, usually hit when the opponent is at the net, and in this case not intended to be an outright winner. It can also be used with the opponent in the backcourt, when a player does not want to risk a drop shot by going too close to the lines or net.

Diversionary tactics. Low-percentage shots used to conceal one's main attack. In using diversionary tactics, an opponent is prevented from concentrating all his efforts on nullifying your most effective shots. The opponent must be prepared to defend in more than one area.

Down-the-line shot. A ball hit parallel with, and reasonably close to, a sideline.

Drills. Carefully planned activities that lead toward improvement in tennis, and do not include the playing of regularly scored matches; usually referring to advanced rally-sustaining procedures, however often used synonymously with the word *exercises* in this book.

Drive. Offensive backcourt stroke hit with a full swing off forehand or backhand, and with slight overspin rather than underspin. A drive can also be flat; however, this is not recommended.

Drop shot. A soft ball, with pronounced backspin, hit barely over the net to produce an outright winner or an error. Preferably hit from inside the baseline and directed near the opponent's sideline.

Drop volley. The same as *touch volley* or *stop volley*. A volleyed ball hit softly, low, and near the net to produce an outright winner or error.

Follow-through. The completion of the swing after the racket strings have left the ball.

Foot fault. A service fault, most often caused by stepping on the baseline, or in the court, while striking the ball. It can also be called when the player takes a walking or running motion before the service delivery.

Forecourt. The area between the service line and the net where a player tries to do most of his volleying or smashing.

Forward swing. The act of bringing the racket forward and toward the net before and during contact, and after the ball is struck. The backswing is the first part of the stroke or serve.

Game plan. A tactical plan that is carefully laid out before the match begins.

Groundstroke. A stroke that is made with either forehand or backhand, after the ball hits the ground. Groundstrokes include drives, slices, loops, dinks, drop shots, and half volleys.

Half volley. A stroke in which the racket contacts the ball immediately after it touches the ground. It is a member of the groundstroke family and a misnomer, as it is not a partial volley. It could be termed a *quick pickup*.

Hitting deep. Hitting a ball near the baseline of the opponent's court so that he cannot easily make an offensive shot.

Hitting short or shallow. Hitting a ball that lands near the net, in the center of the opponent's court. It is often a soft ball that can be easily attacked.

Inside of baseline or service line. A point about a foot or two from the baseline or service line between the line and the net.

Lob. A ball hit high in the air that can be either an offensive or defensive shot.

Loop. A groundstroked ball that is hit with a high tra-

jectory rather than directly toward the opponent's court. It usually reaches a height of ten or eleven feet, and is slightly lower than the offensive lob. If it can be done with accuracy, it is desirable to stroke the loop with overspin.

Match. A tennis contest using official scoring and regulation-match procedures in the playing of points, games, and sets.

Net clearance. The space between the path of the ball and top of the net. Passing shots should be hit with a lower net clearance (closer to net) than most other strokes.

No-man's-land. Backcourt area between the service line and baseline where it is often strategically dangerous for players to position themselves.

On the fly. Hitting a ball before it touches the ground. A volley is a ball hit on the fly.

Open court. The part of the court that is unoccupied by the player. An open court results when a player is maneuvered to one side of the court, creating an opening.

Overhead. A stroke hit directly overhead with a compact service motion. It is the answer to a lob and can either be taken on the fly or allowed to bounce. Also called an *overhead smash* or *smash*.

Overhitting. Taking greater risks than necessary by swinging too fast, and aiming closer to the lines and net than ability allows.

Overlearn. To master a stroke so thoroughly that it can be performed as a whole, without thought for its individual components. An overlearned stroke can also be referred to as *deeply grooved*.

Overspin. The ball's motion, in which the top part of the ball is spinning away from the hitter. After striking the ground, the overspin ball jumps slightly forward and therefore has considerable offensive potential. Groundstrokes and serves are often hit with overspin. *Overspin* and *topspin* are synonymous.

Pace. The speed on the ball. Top players hit with excellent pace.

Passing shot. A groundstroke by a baseliner that is primarily intended to be out of the net man's reach. Also, a low ball hit to the net man which he cannot easily put away for a winner.

Percentage tennis. Tactics that result in winning the maximum number of points; a careful analysis of individual shots. (The term was popularized by Jack Kramer.)

Placement. (a) An outright winner, or unreturnable ball, which a player cannot touch or barely can reach with his racket. (b) A shot directed to a place on the court that the hitter aimed for. Good placement means fine control.

Punishing volley. An angled volley, aimed near the net and short, that is physically tiring to retrieve.

Pusher. A player who strokes a tennis ball so carefully and slowly that at racket contact, the ball is almost being pushed rather than forcefully hit. The beginning pusher acquires additional safety by aiming the ball away from the lines and high over the net.

Rally. To stroke the ball back and forth over the net, either in match play or while drilling. A long rally means many consecutive balls hit either with volleys or groundstrokes.

Range of correctness. The principle that there is more than one specific grip or method used to stroke a tennis ball properly. For example, there are three forehand grips that a great game can be based upon: Eastern, Australian, and Midwestern (between Eastern and Western). There are grips out of the range of correctness that handicap a tournament player, such as a Western service grip, or an extreme backhand grip for volleying.

Ranked player. An outstanding tournament player who is given the honor of a numerical rating for the previous year's play. The player with the best record is number one, the second best is number two, etc.

Retriever. A defensive player primarily concerned with returning the ball rather than placing an opponent at a disadvantage. His strategy is based upon an opponent's missing the shot, rather than making a winner or powerful placement.

Short ball. A ball that can be easily attacked because it lands too close to the net and not close enough to the baseline. As the standard of play becomes better, greater depth of shot is necessary. Occasionally, a well-placed short ball landing near a sideline is an excellent tactical play.

Shot. The end result of hitting any ball except a service. Great players hit many good shots in a match.

Slice. A particular spin placed on a ball. A groundstroke or volley hit with the lower edge of the racket leading. A sliced groundstroke has underspin and a little sidespin. The forward path of the racket creates an angle of less than forty-five degrees to the ground. On the service, *slice* means sidespin that could pull the receiver to his right.

Smash. Same as *overhead smash.*

Stroke. The method of hitting the ball. It is often used synonymously with *form*, and usually refers to groundstrokes and volleys.

Topspin. *See* **Overspin.**

Touch. Control, and the ability to make delicate shots such as soft, angled returns, drop shots, and drop volleys. A player with fine touch almost seems to hit the ball with his hand, rather than with a racket. It is also the ability to be effective without using great pace.

Twist. In this text, *twist* is used synonymously with *American twist.* A served ball hit with overspin and sidespin, resulting in high-bouncing ball that breaks to an opponent's backhand after hitting the ground. It is a safe serve and often makes a fine second service. There is also a reverse twist, which the author does not recommend.

Underspin. The ball's motion in which the top part of the ball is spinning toward the hitter. After striking the ground, the ball stays low and does not hop forward with speed. On a great drop shot the ball hardly goes forward at all. *Underspin* and *backspin* are synonymous.

Volley. A stroke used to hit the ball before it bounces. It includes the sidearm shots but not overheads.

TENNIS-COURT DIAGRAM

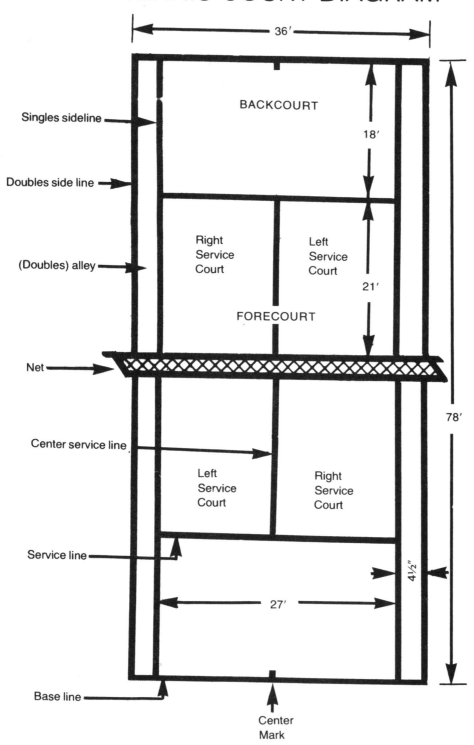

NOTES

NOTES

G.

NOTES

NOTES